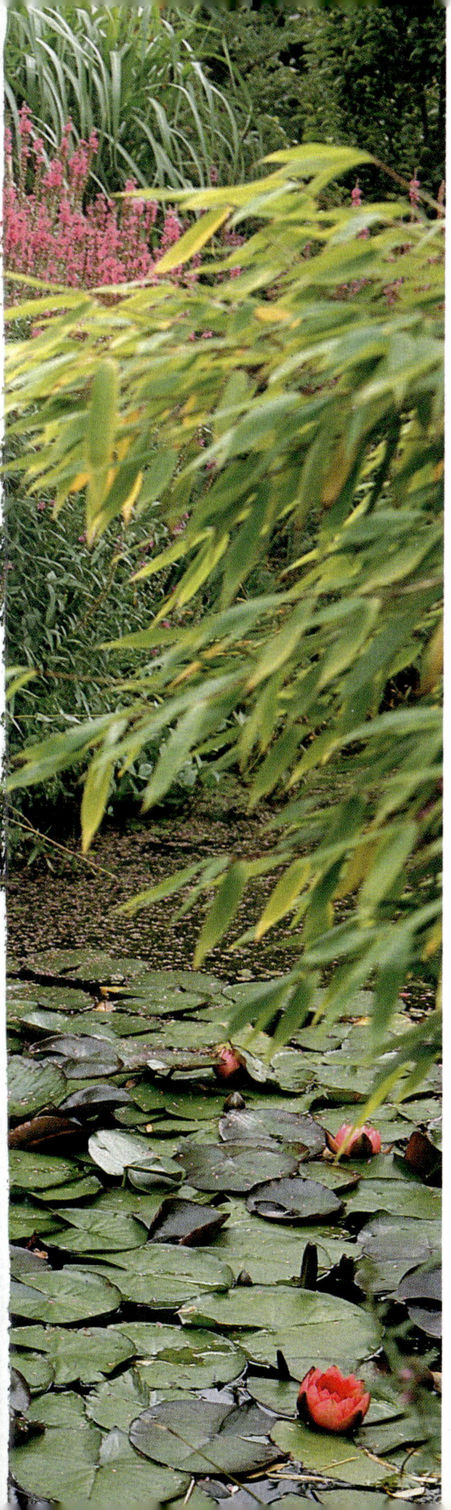

Your
Garden Pond

D1743646

PETER STADELMANN

Series Editor:
LESLEY YOUNG

MEREHURST

Contents

Lysichithum americanum and Primula growing along the course of a stream.

Bulrushes.

A sunbathing frog.

Introduction

Where is the best place to sit and dream in a garden? There can hardly be a more idyllic spot than beside a garden pond, where water lilies unfold their delicate colours, graceful dragonflies hover on the breeze like miniature helicopters and butterflies flutter over the water plants, while down below gleaming goldfish twist and turn, pond skaters hunt for insects, the gentle croaking of a toad can be heard from the marshy depths and a frog sunbathes on a lily pad.

Such a peaceful scene can be created fairly easily in almost any garden and just how to do it is explained by pond expert Peter Stadelmann in this full-colour guide. His clear, detailed instructions will enable any garden owner to design and build their very own pond – be it an ornamental pond with lilies and goldfish, or a wild pond where nature is more or less allowed a free rein. The author offers easy-to-follow instructions for the creation of a pond, from the planning and design stage and digging out of the pit, right through to choosing and planting water plants around the edge of the finished pond. Full-colour step-by-step illustrations demonstrate how to use specific materials for building the pond and show what is needed to create a decorative backdrop. The author has produced a wealth of ideas and inspiration for designing an attractive surround, again with step-by-step illustrations, and there are also extensive suggestions for the planting of attractive marginal and water plants in and around your pond. How to care for a garden pond all the year round is covered in detail, in particular, the measures required for overwintering a pond containing fish. This guide gives advice on which fish will feel particularly at home in a garden pond and how to look after them. If you wish to play host to a large number of wild visitors, like frogs, newts and other amphibians, you will find many tips here on how to provide an ideal environment for such creatures by providing the right food and shelter. This includes the creation of a wild marshy area which has the added attraction of providing a splendid display of flowering and green marsh plants. One chapter is entirely devoted to the particularly attractive idea of creating a running stream, which makes an ideal biological filter and also provides a habitat for plants and animals. Fascinating colour photographs of exceptionally lovely ornamental and wild ponds, as well as photographs of the most beautiful pond plants, fish and other creatures, are sure to inspire the reader to turn their dream of a pond into a reality that can be enjoyed all year round.

The author

Peter Stadelmann is a zoo supplier and also a specialist in the planning, designing, building and stocking of garden ponds.

Warning

Various electrical gadgets and their uses are described in this book. If you are intending to use any of these devices, remember that electrical work of any kind should only be carried out by a qualified electrician. This includes the installation of any kind of electrical gadget as well as laying electrical cables (read the warning about accidents with electrical equipment, p. 36). Make sure that your pond has been made safe for yourself and others (by using protective fencing or railings, see p. 19); this is especially important if there are small children or pets in your household or if the pond is situated in a part of the garden that is not fenced off (see p. 20).

We highly recommend taking out insurance to cover any activities associated with the pond (see liability for accidents associated with garden ponds, p. 20). Every garden pond owner should ensure that no water (either on the surface or underground) is able to penetrate a neighbouring garden. This means regularly checking the water pipes and changing the water in the pond or emptying it in the proper manner (see responsibility for water damage, p. 44).

A garden pond beside a patio
This miniature Eden of water and luxuriant plants invites you to sit and dream.

Forward planning is essential

Even though you are just longing to get started on the physical work, your new pond will turn out far more successfully if you plan it carefully beforehand. The finished pond will be made to measure and any additions, such as a running stream or a marginal marshy area, can be designed in from the very start. One of your chief planning aids will be nothing more sophisticated than a garden hose.

Nature pond or ornamental pond?

If your aim is a pond filled with frogs, newts and other amphibians living together peacefully with colourful goldfish and gleaming koi amid a beautiful display of exotic water lilies by a fountain, you are doomed to disappointment. It is just not possible to combine these three ambitions in one single pond. You will only gain the maximum benefit and pleasure from your pond if you take into consideration the very different basic requirements of individual plants and creatures. This is not very difficult. If your aim is an ornamental pond containing goldfish, koi and other fish, but you also want to coax plenty of wild visitors to take up residence, make sure you plan and build your pond and its surroundings in a way that will meet the requirements of all these creatures. This means that:
● Ornamental fish, which require clear, oxygenated water (see p. 55), will need a larger area of water surface than other creatures.
● Visitors to your garden pond will appreciate an additional habitat in the shape of a marshland or mar-

ginal area beside the pond (see p. 21) or a stream (see p. 50).
On no account should goldfish be introduced *if you want to create a wild pond* which will offer the optimal living conditions for amphibians, dragonflies and countless tiny water creatures, like diving beetles, pond skaters or water fleas. Other fish, like sticklebacks or *Leucaspius delineatus*, are better suited to the life cycle of a nature pond. Some nature pond enthusiasts are of the opinion that no fish at all should be allowed in a wild pond. My own opinion is that a small stock of fish can be kept in a pond that is more than 15 sq m (160 sq ft) in area. My advice is to observe how life develops in your nature pond, check in specialist literature regarding the requirements of those creatures that have established themselves in the pond and then decide on the issue of fish
A wild or nature pond is an individual biotope which should remain undisturbed, if possible. Only a minimum of care will be required and any work should be carried out with some thought (see p. 41).
Both types of pond have one thing in common: they can accommodate

beautiful water plants. The selection of flowering and green water plants is so large that nearly all your preferences can be met in either an ornamental or nature pond.

The size of your pond

Right from the start, you should give some thought to the approximate size of the finished pond and check carefully whether the position you have chosen is suitable for the installation of a pond.
The area of water: It would be almost impossible to give a minimum recommended area.
The basic rule must be that the larger the pond is, the less sensitive it will be to interference. However, let me stress that even a small garden pond, which is all that is generally feasible in most gardens due to lack of space, will still work perfectly well if you design and build it properly and look after it well. You should hardly have any problems with a roundish pond that has an area of about 6 sq m (3 x 2 m or 120 x 80 in). This size is appropriate for ornamental and nature ponds. For any pond with an area of less than 6 sq m (64 sq ft), the possibilities of designing it in an attractive way, stocking it with fish or providing a habitat for other pondlife are fairly restricted.
Depth of the water: One section of the pond – an area of about 1 sq m (11 sq ft) – needs to be at least 70 cm (28 in) deep.
This area of deeper water is essential for fish and other creatures, particularly for overwintering.
NB: If you wish to insert a layer of soil or gravel at the bottom of the pond, the pit will have to be dug 20-30 cm (8-12 in) deeper, so that the necessary depth of water can still be attained later on!
The shape: This has no bearing on

An attractive geometric layout of pond and plants.

the life processes within the pond. Basically, you can choose whatever shape you wish providing it is suitable for the available insulating material (see p. 9).

My tip: A pond can nearly always be built, even in the smallest of gardens. If you have very little space, you may still be able to build a terraced pond, which will enable many beautiful water plants to flourish (see p. 15).

The ideal position

If you are keen on watching pondlife and enjoy growing water plants, it is probably a good idea to choose a position close to a patio or much frequented corner where you often sit. You will, however, have to take into consideration certain factors that are prerequisites for the existence of a healthy, flourishing community of pond creatures and plants.

Take a long garden hose and lay it out at the chosen site in the shape of the pond you are intending to build. Then take a good look at your design with the following points in mind:

Length of exposure to sunlight: light, warmth and, of course, shade are important factors for the growth of plants.

● Note the number of hours during which the site you have chosen will be in shade.

● Ideal: shade during the midday period; exposure to sunlight during the rest of the day.

● The pond must have a minumum of eight hours' exposure to sunlight per day.

● If the chosen position is in intense sunlight all day long, you will have to erect shade providers (hedges, tall-growing edge or bank plants).

Weather influence: The pond should be protected on the side exposed to the prevailing wind (especially if this is to the north or north-west).

The installation of some kind of protection against weather must be designed close to the pond if the wall of a building or other existing plantings do not already offer protection. Good weather protection devices are:

● an earth wall, which can be built with the soil excavated from the pond basin;

● a dense planting, approximately 40-50 cm (16-20 in) tall, around the edge of the pond.

NB: Weather protection can also have a favourable effect on the mini-climate (the climatic conditions in the immediate vicinity) that will develop around the pond. This is important for the growth of the plants and for the living conditions of wildlife in and around the pond.

Trees: If possible, a pond should not be built immediately under trees. If too many leaves and conifer needles are allowed to drop into the water during autumn, they may alter the quality of the water to a point where it begins to endanger the well-being of water plants and pondlife. At a sufficient distance from the pond, however, trees may become welcome providers of shade.

The curious mating display of the azure damselfly (Coenagrion puella).

The frog is a popular visitor to a garden pond.

Soil suitability: A trial trench will give you some idea of the prevailing conditions and tell you whether you will be able to dig down deep enough in the chosen position to provide a depth of at least 70 cm (28 in).

If you come across large pieces of rock or stone, the problem can be solved with the help of some protective material (see p. 14).

● If the subsoil is very rocky, it would be better to construct a pond with a raised water level (see p. 15).

Mains conduits, pipes etc.: Make sure there are no electrical cables or water or drainage pipes near the pit that you dig for the pond. Either your own building plans or the relevant planning office will be able to give you information on the course of mains lines.

My tip: The installation of a garden pond does not normally require planning permission. What you are required to do, however, is to include safety provisions for the protection of children (see p. 19) and to make sure that water is not able to penetrate a neighbouring property (see p. 44).

Room for extending the pond: In my experience you would not be the first gardener who, after completing the construction of a pond, suddenly decided that an area of marshland or a running stream was the one thing they needed to complete their design, and then found there was not enough room for your plans. This is why I recommend giving some thought to this possibility right from the start, so that there will be room, later on, for an attractive extension.

NB: You may also need room for a soakaway which can accommodate pondwater if the water level rises to overflowing level during periods of heavy rain (see p. 18).

Water and electricity

Usually, the pond will have to be supplied with water and electricity from the house. Check before you start whether this is feasible.

Fresh water supply: The simplest solution is to have a sufficiently long, sturdy garden hose to supply water from the house to the pond, laid at about a spade's depth underground.

Electricity and oxygen supply: You will require two PVC pipes for this purpose, with a diameter of about 2.5 cm (1 in) (obtainable in the plumbing trade or from an electrical supplier). These pipes will accommodate electrical cables and an air hose from an air pump (see p. 39). The pipes should be buried at a spade's depth and so that they run slightly downhill from your house. This means laying the pipe a few centimetres deeper at the pond end, so that any moisture in the pipe will run away from the house.

My tip: There are a number of possibilities for conducting electricity to your pond or for installing electrical output units near the pond. The best plan is to obtain advice from a professional electrician.

Warning: Remember that all electrical installations should only be carried out by an expert! I would warn any layperson against installing their own cables or against any do-it-yourself connection of electrical devices. Liability for accidents arising from the use of electricity rests with the person who carried out the work. If you use electrical gadgets in your pond, which would probably be the case in an ornamental pond or a running stream, please read and take note of the safety advice in the section on "helpful gadgets" (see p. 36).

Insulation materials

It is best to decide during the planning phase which insulation material you intend to use in your pond. The most frequently used materials nowadays are PVC lining material or ready-moulded ponds. However, instead, you may wish to use clay as an insulation layer in a nature pond. If you have not already made your decision on this, it might be a good idea to read through the instructions for carrying out the work in the following chapter, so that you have some idea of what is involved. Any mistakes will probably prove expensive to correct and may also spoil your enjoyment of the finished result.

From my own experience, I can offer the following advice:

The easiest materials to work with are various types of pond insulation material (see p. 12). Even those of you who have not had much experience with do-it-yourself projects will find it easy to handle. Using this PVC lining, ponds of any size or shape can be constructed with ease. Using *ready-moulded ponds* is equally problem-free; fibre-glass moulded ponds can be obtained in a wide range of sizes and shapes (see p. 16).

Clay will involve more work and some skill (see p. 18). I would not recommend insulating a pond with roofing felt or fibre-glass reinforced polyester resin. From my own experience of using them in garden ponds, these materials have not proved themselves to be very durable.

You will need the help of an expert if you decide to use *concrete.*

Constructing a garden pond

Now that the planning phase is over and you have decided on the optimum position, shape and size of your garden pond, it is time to get to work. The more meticulous you are in the laying out and construction at this stage, the less planning or alteration will have to be done later on and the better the plants, fish and other creatures will do in your garden pond.

Initial considerations

No matter what insulation material you have decided to use, the following advice will be important for anyone constructing a garden pond.

Excavation work

Do not be too eager to get started and think seriously whether you really want to dig the pit yourself with a spade or shovel. The work involved in excavating a large pit should not be underestimated. I have known even dedicated DIY enthusiasts, who would think nothing of building anything from a raised bed in the garden to a home-made wardrobe, lose all their enthusiasm for a garden pond because the excavation work turned out to be such a backbreaking slog. You can imagine some of the possible consequences of such unaccustomed physical exertion on an unfit person. Blisters on your hands might be the least of your troubles and it is definitely worth avoiding overdoing things and ending up with back problems. Remember, the larger the pond, the greater the quantities of earth that have to be moved. From my own experience, I would suggest the following:

● If you dig out a pond by yourself, only work as long as you really feel up to it at any one session – even if it takes days until the desired size of pit has been excavated. That way, aches and pains can be kept within reasonable bounds.

● Why not invite friends around for a "digging party". In a large group, working together (with something sustaining and delicious to eat and drink afterwards), this rough work will be done much more quickly and it will be more fun too. The finer work, like smoothing the shape of the pond, is best done alone as too many cooks will spoil the broth in this situation!

● The simplest, but also the most expensive, solution is to rent a small excavator from a building firm. However, access for the excavator would be a prerequisite for this alternative.

The pond profile

This is the shape of the pond. What kind of pond profile to use should be decided on before excavating the pit. In the case of a ready-moulded pond, of course, the profile will be predetermined. With all

What you will need for constructing your pond

● small wooden pegs or a garden hose for laying out the shape of the pond;
● three polythene sheets for stacking and storing the grass turves, topsoil and earth you dig up;
● spades, shovels, picks and, maybe, a small excavator for digging out a pit;
● an axe for removing any large roots you may come across;
● a spirit level and a long plank which will reach across the pit (only for small ponds) or a garden hose adapted as a water level (see p. 12);
● insulation materials (PVC liner, moulded pond or clay);
● protective material for use against a hard or stony subsoil;
● lengths of rounded wood or stones for reinforcing the sides of the pond;
● material for constructing the edge of the pond (see p. 22);
● tools: hammer, nails, pliers, screw drivers, crow bar, perhaps a drill.

other materials, you can decide on the depth of the pond and the course of the bank.

The ideal pond profile: The shape is comparable to a soup bowl (see illustration p. 14). This will make reinforcing the soil around the edges of the pond unnecessary. The flat banks of the pond will offer plenty of room for decorative marginal and shallow-water plants.

Wide, flat/shallow edges: This will cut down the risk of accidents involving children and will make it easier for any animals that have accidentallly fallen into the pond to climb out again. This is also a good way to construct a marginal area (see illustration, p. 22).

Steep banks: A pond should not have steep banks all the way round. Should it be impossible, on account of the position of the pond – perhaps against the wall of a raised patio – to install a dish-shaped profile all the way round the pond, the steep bank will have to be reinforced with the help of a drystone wall (illustration p. 23) or with rounded lengths of wood that are buried vertically along the edge.

Plant terraces: These will provide lots of space for planting baskets but their construction will require additional work. They are not absolutely necessary. Any bank can be planted with luxuriant vegetation using special verge matting (see p. 35) or – in the case of a pond lined with PVC – latticed bricks or stones that are stuck to the PVC liner. Some ready-moulded ponds also incorporate a section of plant terraces.

Marginal area (marshy bed): This is an ideal habitat for many animals and plants. Do consider it during your planning stage. The illustrations on page 22 show how to construct it.

Digging out the pit

You will probably have to store the excavated soil on your lawn. In order to protect the lawn, find three large polythene sheets to hold the grass turves, topsoil and excavated earth. Spread out the sheets some distance away from the pond building site.

A waterfall enriches the water with oxygen.

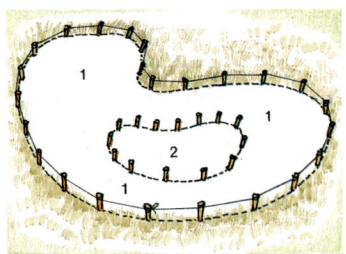

Laying out the shape of the pond
Using string and small wooden pegs, lay out the shape of the pond (1), and also mark out the deep-water area (2).

Method

● First lay out the shape of the pond with the help of small wooden pegs and some string. Do not forget to mark out the different zones or areas, i.e. shallow- and deep-water zones (see illustration above).

● Make spade's-width-sized incisions in the turf, slice the flat turves off, lift them with a garden fork and stack them on the sheet.

● Remove the topsoil and subsoil and heap it separately on large sheets.

My tip: If possible, do not transport the excavated soil away immediately. It might come in useful for constructing a stream course (see p. 50), a waterfall (see p. 24) or for an earth bank (for improving the mini-climate, see p. 8).

Adjusting the water level

In order to prevent your pond running dry later on, like a tipped soup plate, you must make sure the edges of the pond are level.
Method: In the case of a small pond, it will usually be sufficient if you lay a plank, edge upwards, across the edges of the pond and check with a spirit level to see

whether the edges are horizontal. This can be corrected by removing more soil or heaping some back. In the case of a larger pond, take a hose level (made out of a garden hose, see illustration right):

● Stick a small transparent PVC tube into the opening at each end of the hose.

● Fill the hose with water. The hose level functions according to the principle of communicating vessels, which means that the water levels in both transparent end tubes will always be at the same height.

● Lay the hose in the excavated pit. Tie one end of the hose to a post so that you can move around with the other end in your hand. Walk around the edge of the pond and, if necessary, mark out the future edge of the pond with wooden pegs.

● The edge of the pond can be corrected by extra digging or by replacing soil.

How to install a PVC liner

According to many experts, and in my own experience, special PVC lining material is best for the construction of a garden pond.

The right kind of lining material

Only use specially made garden-pond PVC liner for insulating your pond.
Good pond insulation material is made by various manufacturers and is obtainable in the gardening trade.
A guarantee should be given when you buy a good insulating material and, in the case of reputable manufacturers, this guarantee should last for many years. The guarantee should certify that the sheet is:

● UV-resistant (resistant to ultraviolet rays in sunlight);

● resistant to pressure from roots;
● tear-proof;
● heat- and frost-resistant:
● non-degradable;
● naturally, the manufacturers should also guarantee that the PVC does not contain substances nor release substances that are harmful to animals or plants.

My tip: Many manufacturers print their firm's name on the sheeting, so that the source of the insulation material is available if there is cause for complaint.

The thickness of the lining material should not be less than 0.6 mm; a thickness of 0.8-1.0 mm is highly recommended.
The usual colours of commercially available material are anthracite, black, greyish-olive, olive green or earth colour, so that the garden pond will look natural and not take on the appearance of a swimming pool.
Totally unsuitable: the kind of tough polythene sheeting used in the foundations of houses. This is not UV-resistant and contains "softeners", which are released on exposure to sunlight and which quickly make the material brittle and leaky. In the worst types of this sheeting,

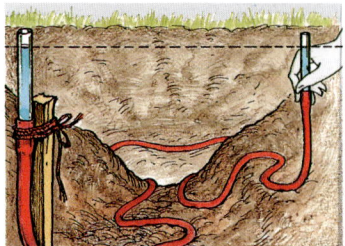

Adjusting the projected water level
You can check whether the edge of the pond (and the future surface level of the water) is horizontal using a water hose level.

the released substances have proved so harmful to animals and plants that the liner has had to be removed from the pond.

How much material is required?
The example calculation below will help you to work out how much insulation material you are going to need, when you insert your own relevant measurements.

Insulation material for ponds can be obtained in various sizes and can be bought by the metre in rolls of different widths. The standard size will usually be sufficient for *small ponds*. This will save you having to glue or heat-weld lengths of insulation material together. It is a good idea to do a rough calculation of the requirements for insulation material for a small pond before you start digging out the pit. Often, minor changes in the projected length or width of the pond will enable you to manage with commercially available sizes of PVC liner. Lay out your garden hose in the desired shape of the garden pond. Measure the length and width as shown in the illustration (right) and use the measurement for the planned depth of the pond. Do not forget to add the necessary extra insulation for the edges of the pond (see calculation below).

In the case of larger ponds, welding together lengths of insulation material will be unavoidable. You can do this yourself or let a manufacturer deliver ready-welded insulation material direct to you. The advantage of this is that the manufacturer will provide a guarantee for the durability of the welded seams (which he would not do if you join them together yourself). You will, of course, incur an additional cost for labour and transport.

My tip: If you are intending to con-

struct a marginal area too, calculate the additional insulation material required as you would for the pond.

Joining lengths of insulation material
There are three ways of joining lengths of insulating material:
● welding the lengths together with an expanding adhesive, using the cold-welding technique. These substances can be obtained in the gardening trade;
● sticking them together using tape or liquid joiner (also obtainable in the gardening);
● hot welding – this method is really only suitable for an expert as a layperson would find it difficult to obtain an absolutely watertight seam.

Warning: Expanding adhesives and other adhesives have to be used with great care as they can be hazardous to health if used in the wrong way! Make sure to observe the following advice:
● follow all instructions exactly;.
● never carry out any work in a closed room;
● wear protective gloves;
● use safety goggles;
● keep naked flames or lit cigarettes well out of the way;

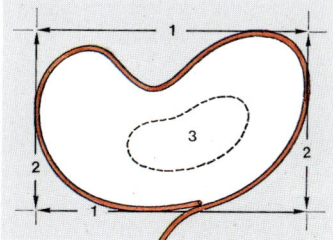

How to work out the quantity of lining material needed
The following measurements will be needed to calculate the amount of lining material needed:
1. The maximum length of the pond;
2. The maximum width;
3. The maximum depth of the deep-water zone.

● the remains of expanding and other adhesives should be disposed of with special waste, not poured down the drain or thrown into your dustbin.

How to glue or weld
It is extremely important to make sure that the areas to be joined are completely free of dirt or dust.
● Lay the lengths of insulation material on a bench or plank so that they overlap by about 5 cm (2 in).

Three important steps when laying the pond lining

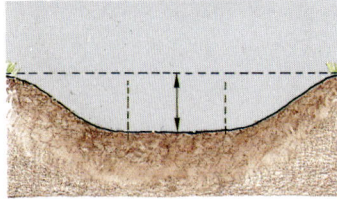

Dig out the pit
It is important to have a pit that measures at least 1 m (40 in) and a deep-water zone of at least 70 cm (28 in).

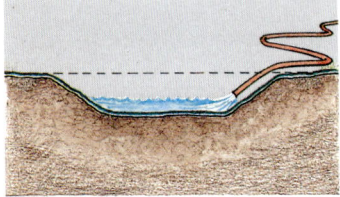

Laying the lining material
First remove any sharp objects from the pit. Next, line the pit with a layer of material that will protect the lining. Then lay out the PVC lining and immediately run water into the pond – very slowly.

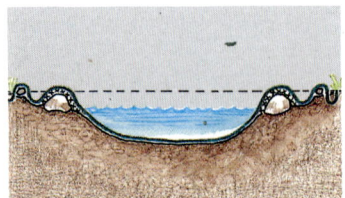

Securing the lining to the edges
Around the edges, draw the lining across stones or rounded sections of wood (cover the stones with a protective layer of material). Bury the lining in the earth so that the edges of the lining are directed upward.

● With a brush, paint the adhesive on to both edges of the insulation material.
● Press down hard on the glued joins with a rubber roller, then weigh down each section with a sandbag for about five to ten minutes.

How to line the pond with the insulating material
Once you have dug a pit for the pond and adjusted the edges (see p. 12), you may continue as follows.
Preparations: Make sure to remove all sharp objects from the pit (such as nails, stones or buried builders' rubble). Any sharp-edged, large, buried rocks should be worked with a hammer and chisel until they are fairly rounded and smooth.
Protective layer: Avoid any damage to the insulation layer from below by first lining the pit with a protective layer of material (obtainable in the gardening trade). If the subsoil is rocky or very stony or simply very hard, first insert a layer of sand in the pit, then lay the protective material over it.
Inserting the insulation layer: The larger the pond, the heavier the insulation material will be – so a couple of strong helpers are highly recommended!
● In the case of small ponds, you can spread out the insulation material beside the pit and then drag it over the pit so that it overlaps the pit by about 30 cm (12 in) on all sides.
● For larger ponds, it is advisable to place the folded material in the centre of the pit, then gradually unfold it towards the edges. Again, it should overlap all around the edges of the pit.
Filling in with water: Immediately after laying down the insulation material, very slowly fill the pond with water, until it is three-quarters full. The water will press the material down into the pit. While the water is rising, you will still be able to get rid

of folds and wrinkles in the material, or adjust them so that they will be less visible. Folds and wrinkles will not adversely affect the durability of the insulation material.
Corrections to the profile of the pond: For small adjustments, merely lift the insulation material at the edge and use sand or soil to correct the mistake. If major corrections become necessary, you will have to lower the level of water by means of a pump.
Reinforcing the bank: Places around the edge of the pond, in particular those which will later be trodden on a great deal, will require reinforcing with stones or lengths of rounded or squared wood. Suggestions for a footpath along the edge of a pond are given on page 22.
Securing the insulation material along the edges of the pond: No matter how you decide to construct the edge of the pond, you will have to secure the insulation material to the edges so that no fine channels of water can form which will deprive the pond of water through capillary action.
● The insulation material should be covered by soil to a depth of about 10-15 cm (4-6 in) around the edges.
● The best way to do this is to draw the material over stones covered with some of the protective layer material or across rounded or squared lengths of wood.
● Place the ends of the material in the soil in such a way that the pull is upwards.
NB: You will find many suggestions for reinforcing the bank and constructing the edges on page 22.

Solving problems

What should you do if your garden is situated on a slope or if the subsoil is so hard that only a pneumatic drill will be able to penetrate to any depth? There are quite simple solutions to both these problems.

A pond lined with insulation material on a slope

The most important point to consider with a pond on a slope is that the soil must not start slipping. The slope must be securely reinforced by means of L-shaped builders' blocks (obtainable from builders' merchants), as shown in the illustrations on the right. Two possible ways of reinforcing the pond on the valley side are also shown on the right.

A lined pond with a raised water level

This method is very suitable for terrain with extremely hard subsoil and for those people who are not so keen on digging. If the deep-water area is planned at, say, 80 cm (32 in), you will only have to dig out this area to a depth of 40 cm (16 in).
Method (see illustration, p. 18)
● Peg out the outline of the pond pit, making sure to indicate the area of deep water as well as the shallow part.
● Bury vertical lengths of rounded wood along the pond edge so that they protrude 40 cm (16 in) above the ground.
● Dig out the deep-water area to a depth of 40 cm (16 in).
● Place the excavated soil behind the rounded lengths of wood to reinforce them.
● Insert the insulation material. Nail the edges of the insulation material to the wood and then bury it in the earth bank so that the edges of the material are pointing upwards.
● If the earth bank is going to be walked on later, reinforce the relevant section by means of a drystone wall (see illustration, p. 18).
● Plant the earth wall or bank with the kind of plants that will form a good rooting system to consolidate the bank.

A pond in front of a patio wall

If you wish to be able to view the pond from your patio, you will need to build it right beside the patio wall. Very often, a steep bank will be created that will require reinforcing with a drystone wall.
Method (see illustration, p. 18)
● After digging the pit for your pond, you will have to build a foundation for the drystone wall. This can be laid in concrete or you may obtain ready-made foundation stones from your local builders' merchant.
● The drystone wall is erected by placing the bricks together without mortar! If necessary, fill any cracks or uneven sections between the bricks with soil.
● It will be absolutely necessary to insert a protective layer of material between the drystone wall and the layer of insulation material. The same goes for the patio pavingstones, which may lie on top of the insulation material around the edge of the pond.

A patio pond

Some gardens are so small that there would be no room for a lawn or flowerbed if you wanted to install a pond. However, the owners of such gardens can still consider the possibility of constructing a pond on the patio. You will need lengths of squared wood and insulation material.
Method
● You can obtain squared wood of different lengths in builders' yards. Some types of wood are prepared in such a way that they only need to be slotted together in the desired position.
● Drill holes vertically into the joins with a 10-mm wood drill.

Building a pond on a slope; reinforcing the slope and valley sides

Dig out the slope
Dig out the slope to a depth of about 70 cm (28 in).

Reinforce the slope side
Secure the soil to stop it from slipping by using L-shaped stones. Lay the lining, weigh it down with lattice bricks or stones and, using silicon adhesive, glue it to the L-shaped stones.

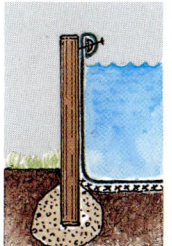

Securing the valley side
Left: Sections of rounded wood are sunk into a foundation of ready-made concrete. Wrap the lining around a small rounded piece of wood and nail it to the large section of wood.
Right: Bury the rounded wood at least 40 cm (16 in) deep. Construct a drystone wall and secure the lining to it with the help of a wooden batten, screws and countersunk screws. Lay a plank loosely across the top.

● Then hammer in bolts (obtainable from an ironmongers). If the pond is situated on soil, the bolts must be long enough to be firmly anchored in the soil beneath the wood.

● If the pond is built on patio pavingstones, the bolts need only reach down as far as the pavingstones without penetrating them.

NB: Some wood merchants stock ready-made kits for constructing patio ponds of certain sizes, for example, 2.15 m (86 in) long, 1.25 m (50 in) wide and 60 cm (24 in) deep. Once clad with insulation material, these ponds will hold about 1,600 litres (352 gal) of water.

Important: The joined lengths of wood will have to withstand a considerable pressure of water. Make sure, therefore, that the joins are strong and secure. Obtain advice when buying the wood. Many woodyards sell suitable reinforcement materials.

A patio pond is very easy to look after. All you need to do is replenish evaporated water and remove withered parts of plants.

The ege of the pond should be surrounded with low-growing water plants such as miniature water lilies, pickerel weed (*Pontederia cordata*), lobelia, water lettuce (*Pistia stratiotes*) or water plantain (*Alisma plantago*). Watercress, chives and monkey flower (*Mimulus*) will flourish in shallow bowls around the edge. Do not put any soil on the bottom of the pond. The plants should be placed in the pond in baskets.

Fish can only be introduced if you equip your patio pond with the technical accessories of a large cold-water aquarium.

How to install a ready-made pond

The selection of commercially available ready-moulded ponds is quite large. Good manufacturers will also guarantee that the material is harmless to animals and plants and, in addition, UV-resistant, non-degradable, frost-resistant and shock-proof.

The range of different shapes should cater for almost every conceivable wish, from rectangular to oval to L-shaped and kidney-shaped ponds – there should be something to suit every taste.

A division into different sections is particularly useful in larger ponds. These are equipped with several planting terraces and deep- and shallow-water areas. Some ready-made ponds even have a so-called biotope edge, which is a special bay-like section for planting edging plants.

The size of ready-made ponds ranges from small ponds with a capacity of about 100 litres (22 gal) to really large ones that are divided into sections and can hold several thousand litres.

Installing a moulded pond is really quite simple, except that you need to be more exact in digging out the pit than with the insulated type. The more curved the edges of the pond are, the more difficult installation will turn out to be. A ready-made pond must be installed evenly or the water will be tilted in the basin. This is visually unattractive as well as making the pond liable to overflow at one side.

Installing large ready-made ponds that are designed in sections is not quite as easy as the installation of a single basin.

Making the pond pit

● Peg out the outline of the prospective pond. This will be easier if the manufacturer has supplied a template of the pond. If not, stand the moulded pond on the proposed site and draw round the shape with a stick. Then add about 15 cm (6 in) all the way round. This is the margin you will need for washing soil around the edge of the pond.

My tip: Moulded ponds are very stable but it will still be necessary to remove stones, roots and other sharp objects from the pit.

● First dig out the pit for the deepest part of the pond. It should be 15 cm (6 in) wider and 5-10 cm (2-4 in) deeper than the actual moulded pond.

● Cover the floor of the pit with a 5-10 cm (2-4 in) thick layer of sand. The sand should be shaken down by tapping it with the flat blade of a spade so that it forms an even surface.

● Now dig out the rest of the pegged-out area and cover it with a layer of sand.

● Insert the moulded pond and adjust the top edge so that it is completely horizontal. Two planks and a spirit level will be useful for this operation.

How to wash in soil: The hollow spaces round the pond and any remaining hollow spaces underneath must be filled with soil or sand washed in with water. This will prevent the pond from sinking or tilting later on.

● First fill the spaces round the deepest part of the basin with sand and press the sand down with the end of a plank.

● Then – very important! – fill the deepest section with water (let it run in very slowly).

● Let the water run slowly over the sand so that it becomes evenly distributed.

King cups (Caltha palustris)
These are the heralds of spring among pond plants. Their golden yellow flowers begin to appear in mid-spring.

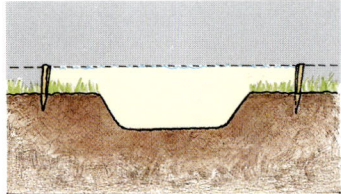 

Building a pond with a raised water surface
Left: Lay out the shape of the pond and mark out the deep-water zone.
Right: Bury rounded sections of wood in an upright position around the edge of the pond so that they protrude about 40 cm (16 in) from the ground. Pile up the soil excavated from the pit behind the wood. Line the pond with a protective layer and PVC liner. Nail the edges of the liner to the wood.

● After that, wash soil or sand into the remaining hollow spaces, while allowing water to run slowly into the pond, gradually adding soil and water, if necessary.

A clay-lined pond

Some nature pond enthusiasts prefer clay for lining a pond. It can usually be obtained from builders' merchants but may be difficult to come by in some areas.
Method: The pit for the pond must be lined with a layer of clay approximately 30 cm (12 in) thick.
● First, distribute the crumbly-dry clay evenly in the pit and then wet it.
● Lightly knead it with your feet or a trowel.
● The idea is to build up a layer of clay that is as evenly distributed as possible and about 30 cm (12 in) thick.
● Next, add a 10-cm (4 in) thick layer of coarse sand. This will prevent pond creatures from churning up the clay later on and making the water cloudy.
● Finally, slowly fill the pond with water. To begin with, some of the water may drain away but this should soon cease as the cracks and fissures will rapidly close up.

● You will need slightly less clay if you insert unfired brick rubble (obtainable from a builder or brickworks) as a base under the clay.

My tip: Pliable clay bricks are available and can be worked like Plasticine. They are fitted together by means of toothed edges and then the joins are covered with a special substance or pressed together.

A run-off

If the water level rises due to heavy rainfall and the pond water runs over the edge, many garden owners allow the overflow to run away into the garden. This avoids the construction of a water run-off and in many cases it will be sufficient. Sometimes, however, the ground cannot cope with the volume of surplus water, so that the surroundings remain very wet for a long time or the water may run into a neighbouring garden (which could cause damage and give your neighbours grounds for complaint). In cases like this, a soak-away will have to be built to carry surplus water into deeper levels of soil before it can spill over the edge of the pond and flood the garden.

For this, you will need a composting basket and enough fist-sized stones to fill the basket.
Method (see illustration, p. 19)
● Dig a hole deep enough to accommmodate the wire basket.
● Line the walls of the basket (not the floor!) with PVC liner and fill the basket with the stones.
● A connection between the pond and the soak-away is formed by means of a section of gutter or a PVC pipe.
● If you need to walk across the soak-away, cover it with wooden boards.

My tip: As a rule, the simple soak-away described above will be adequate. If problems continue to occur, very often only a proper drain into the main sewer will help. In such cases, it will be necessary to consult a sewer or drainage expert.

NB: Please read the advice given on filling and changing water on page 44.

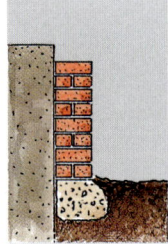 

A pond beside a patio wall
Left: Build a drystone wall on a foundation against the patio wall. Right: Lay a rounded section of wood on the drystone wall. Install the protective layer and the PVC liner. Insert a layer of sand between the liner and the patio paving-stones. Glue the stones to the liner with silicon adhesive.

Safety precautions for the protection of children

Any body of water, along with the creatures living in it, attracts children like a magnet. It is not possible to explain to small children that they may drown in a garden pond. If you really do not wish to delay the construction of a garden pond until your children are older and more sensible, you will need to provide safety barriers around the pond. Flat banks alone will not be sufficient as a safety precaution. You should secure the pond all the way around but must definitely make safe any kind of steep bank.

A protective grid in the pond

A protective grid is a very practical and almost invisible solution. Plants can grow through the grid and any fish living in the pond will not feel in the least disturbed by it. It can be removed again quite easily later on.

Method
● You will require a frame, with wire mesh nailed to it, which is as wide and long as the surface of the water (obtainable in hardware stores).
● The mesh should not be wider than 6-7 cm (2½-2¾ in), and must be rust-proof (get advice from your dealer).
● The grid can be supported on stacked bricks.
● Stack the bricks in such a way that the grid lies about 10 cm (4 in) horizontally below the surface of the water. Make sure it cannot tip up if a weight is applied on one side!

My tip: Any uneven places between the bricks and the bottom of the pond can be smoothed out with silicon adhesive.

Protective fencing

Fences simply invite children to climb them, so they are not quite as safe as a grid in the pond. If you do decide on a protective fence, however, you can do a few things to make it more difficult for human monkeys to scale it.

A fence around the dry edge of the pond (in grass or a flowerbed)
● A wooden fence that is at least 60 cm (24 in) high is very suitable. It should have slats that run vertically. You may purchase sections of ready-made fencing with slats from wood merchants.
● The top ends of the slats should be rounded!
Warning: A cross lattice fence is completely unsuitable as the rather sharp tops of the slats may injury children badly, while the cross lattice itself is just another invitation to climb. Finally, some children may decide to poke their heads through the diamond-shaped holes of the lattice and then find themselves unable to extract them again.
● When buying the fence or the materials to build one, make sure that the substance used to treat the wood does not contain harmful additives which might be washed out by rain and end up in the pond.

I recommend materials that are marked as being environmentally safe.
● If you are going to treat the wood of the fence yourself, do not use substances that will kill plants or harm fish if they leak into the pond.
● Allow the fence to act as a support for luxuriantly growing plants like runner beans, mint, lemon balm, nasturtium or nettles. This will also discourage children from climbing it.

For a marginal area (see p. 21)
The best solution here is a chicken-wire fence.
● For posts, use angle irons of the desired height that have been cemented into large flowerpots.
● Bury the pots in the subsoil.
● Fix plastic-coated chicken wire to the posts.
Warning: The width of the mesh should be 10 cm (4 in) so that birds can fly through it. Small-mesh fencing wire near a pond can become a lethal trap for birds. Use reed-like plants such as bulrushes or grasses to mask the fence.

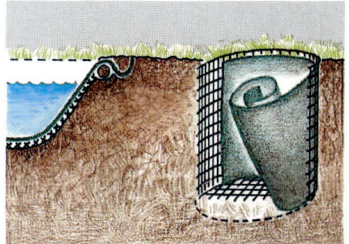

Building a soak-away
Left: Bury a composting wire-mesh basket. Line the walls (not the floor) with PVC liner.
Right: Fill the pit with large stones. Lay a gulley, lined with PVC liner, from the pond to the pit. Cover the pit with boards.

A goldfish pond with a wooden footbridge, harmoniously blended into a colourful, flowering rockery.

My tip: Build a small play pond for your children. A very shallow plastic moulded pond can be buried in the ground and a large pile of sand beside it, for building castles, will be an invitation to paddle and play and will probably distract small children from the more dangerous attraction of the garden pond. Tiny children should not play unsupervised near water, no matter how shallow!

Liability for accidents

Most garden owners will be very aware of the safety of their own children. Many, however, will not be so aware of the fact that certain safety precautions must be taken to ensure the safety of other persons (strangers, visitors, etc). Comprehensive information on legal liability cannot be given within the constraints of this small volume but the garden-pond owner should be alert to the question of health and safety precautions.

What you should know: If the garden pond is within a fenced-off area of garden, the garden-pond owner may assume that no unauthorized persons will intrude on to their land. However, if this does happen, and there is an accident, the injured intruder might wish to sue the pond owner and it would be wise to consult a solicitor as to where one would stand. If the garden pond is situated in an unfenced-off front garden, the garden pond owner must take all reasonable precautions to preserve a third party from accidents.

Warning: If there is any risk of children or adults falling into a garden pond which has not been secured properly in a front garden, you should take steps to put this right. In law, extremely high demands are very often made on an individual's duty to provide safety for others. I highly recommend taking out special insurance with reference to the garden pond. When doing this, you should give a detailed and exact description of the position of the pond and any safety devices provided, and obtain written confirmation from the insurance company that these measures are adequate and any remaining risk is covered by the insurance policy.

Safety precautions for animals

Small mammals, like hedgehogs, mice and pets, frequently fall into a pond. Steep banks and overly smooth edging material, like PVC liner or moulded ponds, can become veritable death traps if the animal cannot find anything to hold on to when trying to climb out. There are several simple measures that will enable animals to escape from a pond.
● Build a hedgehog ladder or install a gently sloping plank.
● Fix a few thick branches to the edge of the pond so that they jut out into the water but do not tip in.
● Lay out a "bathing mat", made of hemp or a similar material, along the edge of the pond so that the mat can be half-buried along the edge or under the grass turves. Weigh the mat down in the pond with stones. Plant creeping-Jenny (*Lysimachia nummularia*) on both sides of the mat so that it grows over the mat and, in time, you will hardly be able to see it.

Designing interesting surroundings

Once the pond itself has been built and filled with water, it is time to think about designing a decorative surrounding. This is not the only way to make your pond look attractive, however. A marginal area, a fountain, bridge, stepping stones, even lighting are further ways to enhance your pond. Choose something that will not only make your pond beautiful but will be practical or sensible for the particular site.

A marginal area

In the wild, the marshy marginal area around a pond is a biologically delimited part of the shallow zone, with its own plant and animal life. In a natural pond, the shallow-water zone ranges very gradually from a depth of about 25 cm (10 in) to 0 cm where it becomes a wet, marshy area.
In order to create a similar marginal area beside a garden pond, the pond would have to be very large (over 15 sq m or 161 sq ft). However, even with a small garden pond you will be able to imitate nature to a certain degree by creating a marshy area on the edge. This will provide a habitat for marginal plants and many animals will find shelter and food here.
The ideal solution is a marginal area for ornamental ponds that contain goldfish and other ornamental fish. As already mentioned on page 6, you cannot expect to find very many pond visitors, such as frogs, toads and newts in that kind of pond. The needs of ornamental fish and the other pond creatures vary far too much. A marginal area that is not too small may help to balance

these differences a little. However, please remember that a combination of an ornamental pond and a marginal area is not the same as a nature pond.

How to create a marginal area
If you have made your pond with lining material, the marginal area can be created in the same way as the pond. The illustrations on page 22 show two possibilities for creating a marginal area with PVC liner insulation material. In the case of a *ready-made moulded pond*, you may still use insulation material or install a specially formed basin right beside the pond (90 x 60 cm or 36 x 24 in; depth 25 cm or 10 in). This basin is designed in such a way that it will always be supplied with water from the pond.
Please note the following points:
● The larger the marshy area, the better it will fulfil the requirements as a habitat for wildlife. An area of about 1-2 sq m (10½-21½ sq ft) is about right (depth 20-25 cm or 8-10 in).

A marginal area with a soil bottom
Line the area with PVC liner. Pile up stones between the pond and the marginal area and glue them to the liner. Fill the hollow with soil.

● The border between the pond and the marginal area should lie partially under the water's surface so that a water supply from the pond is maintained.
● Stack the stones between the pond and the marginal area in such a way that small caves are formed which will serve as shelter for animals. Fix them with silicon adhesive. Also glue the stones to the insulation material beneath.
● It will not harm the plants very much if the marginal area dries out briefly on the odd occasion. If there is a longer period of drought, however, an ornamental pond will have to be topped up anyway.

A marginal area with baskets
Insulate with PVC liner. Glue the stones between the pond and the marginal area to the liner. Put the plants in planting baskets.

● A sand-clay mixture is suitable for the bottom of the pond. This will provide a lime-containing soil, which is what many marginal plants require. You can choose from a large number of plants for *stocking your marginal area.*
● The plants can be planted directly into the bottom if all plants have the same requirements.
● Put any plants with special requirements in baskets, i.e. if your marginal area contains lime-rich soil, plants that require acid or lime-poor soil will have to be placed in baskets – or vice versa.

My tip: Plants that grow luxuriantly should always be set in planting baskets and the baskets themselves sunk into the soil. This will prevent the weaker plants from being smothered.

Designing the edge of the pond

Designing the edge of the pond is a matter of taste. Some people like a pond they can walk right round, others prefer an edging that is planted. A combination is probably most practical for either an ornamental or nature pond. If part of the edge can be walked on, you will be able to observe any pondlife from close up and the pond will be accessible to any measures of care you might have to undertake. The other part, where you cannot walk, will be left completely undisturbed for plants and animals.

An edge that can be walked on
There is a large choice of materials and designs.
Pavingstones, like those used for paths or patios, will need a hard base.
● The steeper the edge of the pond, the harder and more stable

Pavingstones along a flat bank
Reinforce the edge with stones, cover the stones with protective material, then draw the liner over them, directing the edges of the liner upwards. Put a layer of sand on top.

the base will have to be. If you have a steep bank, a drystone wall should be constructed (see illustration, p. 23), otherwise the bank may begin to give way or sink over a period of time if you walk on it.
● Lattice bricks are best for the drystone wall but you can use ordinary red bricks or medium-sized stones.
● In the case of low banks, large stones (or squared pieces of wood) will be sufficient as a base (see illustration above).
Important: Do not place stones immediately on top of any insulation material! Insert a layer of sand, about 5 cm (2 in) thick, between the insulation and the stones. To prevent the sand from seeping into the pond, create a barrier of silicon adhesive between the stones and the insulation (see illustration, p. 23).
Natural stones (obtainable in the building trade) look particularly attractive around a pond. Here, too, a stable base will be necessary. The most suitable types are a drystone wall or large stones and squared pieces of wood.
Wood is a very popular material for designing the edge of a pond.
● Bury rounded pieces of wood standing upright (nail the insulation

material to the wood) and arrange pavingstones, natural stones or a gravel layer behind them.
● Try building a wooden footbridge resting on rounded pieces of wood (see photo, p. 20).
● Secure the edge of the pond with squared wood (see illustration right).
Important: Any wood that you use near or in a pond must not be treated with substances that are harmful to animals or plants. Toxic substances used for treating wood, or other harmful substances, could be washed out by the pondwater or by rain to poison the pond. Do not use old railway sleepers; they have usually been painted with large quantities of anti-woodworm agent, herbicide, etc.

A edge that is not intended to be walked on

Plants and stones are both useful for decorating the edge of a pond.
Verge matting (see illustration, p. 24) is an ideal solution if you want an invisible transition from pond plants to edge plants. In addition, they will cover the insulation material or ready-made pond walls between the surface of the water and the edge of the pond. Various manufacturers produce verge matting made of coconut fibre or woven plastic. The mat is filled with suitable soil (see p. 27) and planted. The soil will

not be able to slip into the pond and the roots of the plants will have plenty of support. Verge matting with planting pockets is particularly useful. The pockets can be filled with soil, so that even steep banks can be effortlessly planted.
Important: The matting is secured with special hooks but they should never, either in the pond or around the edge, be poked through the insulation material. Always affix the hooks outside the insulation material. The matting can be weighed down with gravel.

A small marshy ditch along the edge of the pond.

● Dig out soil to a width of 30-40 cm (12-16 in) at the edge of the pond and at the same level as the surface of the water.
● Lay the insulation material over the ditch you have dug then draw it over some rounded pieces of wood and allow the edges of the material to stand up vertically (to stop moisture seeping away into the garden).
● Lay stones along the edge of the pond (right beside the water). If necessary, glue heavy stones to the insulation material with silicon adhesive so that they are unable to tip over into the pond.
● Fill the marshy ditch with soil and plant marginal plants in it.
A stone wall along the edge of the pond is a simple and very attractive

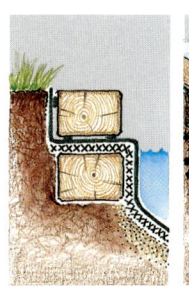

Edging made of squared wooden sections
Lay a protective layer, then the liner over the bottom sections of squared wood. Lay the top sections on top and glue them to the liner. To secure the joints, drill through the wood and drive in bolts.

feature. In the case of an insulated pond, light-weight stones should be glued to the material with silicon adhesive to prevent them from slipping.
A lawn or flowerbed may reach right to the edge of the pond.
● If you have not already done so when you dug the pit for the pond, now remove a width of grass turf to a depth of about 7 cm (2¾ in) or remove soil from a flowerbed.
● Draw the insulation material across the edge of the pond so that it overlaps by about 30 cm (12 in) (make sure the edges of the material stand up vertically).
● Lay the turf you removed earlier (or flowerbed soil) on the insulation layer. The grass turves will soon grow together again.
● In the area on top of the insulation layer, a moist zone will now be created in which shrubs can flourish. This area should not be confused with a proper marginal area which will always be supplied with pond water by virtue of its design (see p. 21). The plants that grow here will not cope with constant waterlogging, unlike marginal plants.

Pavingstones and a drystone wall providing a path along a steep bank

Pile up stones, filling the cracks with soil (do not use mortar). Lay a protective covering between the wall and the liner. Install a layer of sand, then apply a thick layer of silicon adhesive between the paving stones and the liner.

A pond edge with verge matting and plants

Pull a protective layer and then PVC liner over stones at the edge. Bury the liner so that a gulley is formed which will be filled with gravel. Lay the verge matting in such a way that it is secured by the gravel or secure the verge matting behind the liner with special hooks sunk into the soil. Do not drive the hooks through the liner. Fill the matting with soil and insert the plants.

A waterfall

A waterfall beside your pond will offer several advantages, for example:
● The water flowing down will become enriched with oxygen and will supply the pond with extra oxygen.
● The gentle trickling sound of the water may neutralize traffic noise – at any rate, the trickling of water is much more pleasant than the roar of traffic.
● If you wish to combine the waterfall with a running stream, the waterfall can form the mouth of the stream (see p. 50).

How to build a waterfall
You can build a waterfall at the same time as you dig out the pit for a pond (see illustration, p. 25). You will need pond insulation material, three pavingstones, a few roof tiles, silicon adhesive and soil (a mixture of sand and clay in a ratio of 1:3 or 1:4).
● The height and width of the waterfall will depend on the size of the pavingstones.
● Pile up the soil you have excavated into a mound, making it high enough to embed the three pavingstones in it.
● Cut a step into the mound.

● On the side facing the pond, cover the mound up to the top with insulation material and then draw this over a rounded piece of wood at the top.
● Bury all the edges of the insulation material in the soil so that they point upwards.

My tip: If the insulation material you have used to line the pond is not long enough, connect the material you are going to use for the mound by welding it so that no water can seep through it.

● Arrange roofing tiles on the step in the mound in such a way that the pavingstones can be laid on top, angled slightly downwards.
● Lay the pavingstones on top and secure them with silicon adhesive.
● The water used for the fall should be pondwater: a garden hose should be inserted into the pond, connected to a waterpump and then laid up to the top of the mound.
● Cover the hose and the insulation material with stones.
● Plant colourful summer flowers (day lily, calendula, marsh marigold or grasses) on the mound. It is also ideal for a small rockery.

My tip: You will be able to make a waterfall even quicker if you spread out a piece of insulation material at the edge of the pond (weld it to the pond insulation layer) and pile up some stones on it. Lay the garden hose between the stones so that it points upwards. This will give the effect of a spring.

More ambitious waterfalls
There are endless ways of making waterfalls.
Stones in many sizes, shapes and colours can be arranged to form steps for the water to flow down. *A series of steps can be made out of a varied range of small basins* (made of plastic or ceramic) which can be obtained in the gardening trade.
NB: The more elaborate your waterfall, and the heavier the material, the more stable the base will need to be. A loosely piled up mound will not be solid enough to support heavy stone steps or ceramic basins.
● For this you will have to bury a framework of upright, rounded pieces of wood or, even better, build a step-like solid drystone wall.
● The mound is then piled on top of this base and the path of the waterfall secured with pond insulation material.
● Heavy stone steps and basins should be secured with cement (never with lime-based mortar).

My tip: Make sure the slope (or the individual steps) of the waterfall is not too steep. In a nature pond, or even in an ornamental pond containing fish, it is not exactly beneficial to pondlife to have water gushing down with great force and a lot of noise on to the surface of the pond.

Various types of fountains

In addition to a waterfall, there are other ways of introducing moving water into your pond. From a water spout to a regular fountain, devices for spraying water are available in the gardening trade in the most imaginative variations. It is, however, quite easy to overdo things. If water is bubbling, squirting and trickling in every nook and cranny of your pond, the plants will not flourish so well and the fish will not like it much either. Visitors, like frogs and newts, may even "emigrate".
Stick to these three basic rules:

● A small pond should have only a small waterfall.

● At most, a nature pond will only put up with a gently bubbling fountain or a spring stone at the edge of the pond (see illustration right).

● Large fountains should not be installed in ponds that contain fish and water lilies. If you really do want a fountain among water lilies, make sure the water does not trickle down on to the lily pads.

Water spouts, spring stones and small fountains

A large selection is available in the gardening trade, installation is usually quite a simple affair and there will be something for every taste and purse. If you have a pond with plants and pondlife, the running water should not be switched on all the time. The best idea is to switch it on only when you are actually spending time at the pondside. A practical solution is to connect a small fountain to the mains for additional fresh water. The alternative is to run the fountain with pondwater and a small waterpump.

Water spouts are available in various different materials – from plastic to ceramic to sculpted sandstone – shaped like frogs, garden gnomes or cherubs.

● A water spout should be placed on the edge of the pond in a manner that will prevent it from tipping into the pond.

● Protect the insulation layer by inserting a piece of suitable material between the layer and the water spout.

● If the figure is very heavy, a dry-stone wall should be built under-

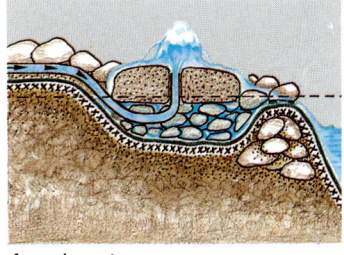

A spring stone
Dig a shallow pit at the edge of the pond and line it with protective material and PVC pond liner. Fill the hollow with stones and set the spring stone on top. Thread the water hose through the hole in the spring stone.

neath it or it can stand on rounded pieces of wood buried vertically.
Spring stones are often boulders with a chiselled hole. They can be obtained in different sizes, made of natural or synthetic stone.

● They may be set in shallow water or in a separate basin beside the pond so that the water can run into the pond.

● In the gardening trade, DIY kits can be obtained, which include a spring stone, a basin (insulation material or squared wood) and stones for filling the basin.
Small fountains can be placed in the pond, fixed to a lattice brick and fed by a waterpump. They are less overpowering than a large fountain; water falling from a minimal height will not disturb pondlife so much.

A large fountain

A large fountain has no business in a nature pond. Do not try it in an ornamental pond with fish and water lilies either. If you really do hanker after both a pond and a large fountain, my advice is to install the fountain in a separate basin. Too large a fountain can actually cause damage to a pond!

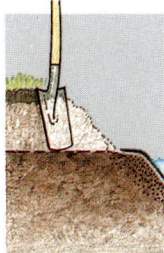 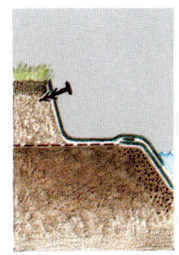 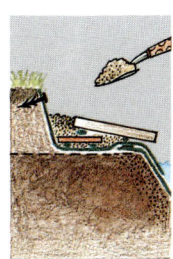 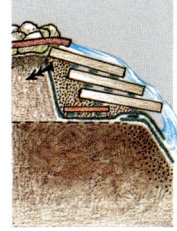

Building a simple waterfall
Pile up a mound at the edge of the pond and dig out a step. Cover the entire mound to the top with PVC liner, making sure the liner is as wide as the waterfall. Anchor the liner in the soil or draw it across rounded wood sections at the top. Glue the liner to the edge of the pond. Tilt the first pavingstone at an angle on several roofing tiles and secure it with silicon adhesive. Fill the spaces with sand. The other pavingstones should be laid on in steps and glued to each other with silicon adhesive. Connect the water hose.

Cross-sections of treetrunks used as stepping stones.

The constant hard splashing down of water from a high fountain causes great stress for fish, which have extremely sensitive organs along their sides for registering pressure waves. Such incoming signals are then passed on to the brain. This could be compared to the effect of a person being constantly tickled without being able to escape from their tormentor. The fish will eventually die of massive overstimulation.

The leaves and flowers of water lilies will probably not be damaged by drops of water falling on them but if they are constantly wet they will be unable to extract vital gases from the air and will deteriorate and die after a short time.

The pondwater is constantly pushed through minute openings in the fountain's jet and is swirled about so fiercely that micro-organisms living in the water begin to die. The result is that the biological balance in the pond is quite severely disturbed.

NB: You may find complete fountain building kits in the gardening trade, complete with insulation material, pump shaft, pump, fountain attachments and a cover for the pump shaft.

My tip: Foam bubblers should always be installed in a separate basin. If they are put in a garden pond containing wildlife, the water will begin to smell rotten after a very short time. This is caused by algae rapidly multiplying in the vicinity of the bubbling device but the algae can usually only be eradicated with the help of harmful chemicals.

Footbridges, stepping stones and lights

These decorative elements really belong to a more sophisticated type of garden pond design. They will involve a great deal of time and work and are rather expensive too.

Footbridges made of wood, natural sandstone or concrete can be obtained in almost all sizes in the gardening trade, in wood merchants and in some builders' yards. The degree of difficulty involved in their installation will depend largely on the size and weight of the bridge. A solid foundation (made of concrete or wood) will usually be necessary.

Stepping stones will make it possible to walk across the pond. They are very practical in the case of large ponds as they will make routine care in or around the pond a great deal easier. The stepping stones should be placed on solid concrete pillars. I advise getting help from an expert when it comes to installing these.

My tip: Builders' yards can usually provide U-shaped stones (from 40 cm or 16 in upward) which make excellent bases for stepping stones. Fix the stepping stone to the base with silicon adhesive. Be very careful with the U-shaped stones, however, as they have rather sharp edges, so laying a couple of layers of insulation material between the base and the stepping stone, to act as padding, is a good idea.

Lights beside, or even in, the pond will create a magical atmosphere on warm summer evenings. You may even find floating, globe-shaped lamps on the market, which can be anchored to the bottom of the pond. An underwater cable forms a connection to the mains.

NB: Remember that all electrical installations should be carried out by an expert (see p. 36)! The lamps can also be used with low-voltage electricity (see p. 38).

Plants around your pond

Growing plants around the garden pond will help to create a natural look. The plants should be green and in flower from spring to autumn, and this is quite possible if you choose the right plants. The amount of time you will need to spend on caring for the plants will be minimal during the summer months, so you will still have time to enjoy the pond.

Soil for the pond and planting baskets

Nature pond enthusiasts will probably decide from the start to install a proper layer of soil at the bottom of the garden pond. In the case of an ornamental pond, however, which will usually contain fish such as goldfish or koi, a layer of soil would soon become churned up so that you would be unable to see the pondlife anymore. Planting baskets are more practical for this situation (see p. 35). Whether you choose to use planting soil in baskets or a layer of soil at the bottom of the pond, the decisive factor for the well-being of plants and pond creatures will always be the constituents of the soil mixture. A badly composed mixture can considerably interfere with life in a pond.

Basic rules for the right soil
● The soil mixture should be poor in nutrients.
● Most garden soils or humus made with compost are too rich in nutrients. These soils may cause algae to flourish (see p. 45) or even create an imbalance in the chemical content of the water.
● Fertilized soils will introduce substances to the pond that also

encourage the formation of algae.
● A layer of pure gravel is not the ideal solution either as debris will become lodged in it and biologial decomposition processes will be activated in the tiny pockets between the pieces of gravel. The nutrients thus liberated remain concentrated in the gravel layer to begin with and are then released into the water as welcome food for algae and other single-cell lifeforms. Overproduction of algae, cloudy water and even layers of slime on the surface of the water will be the result.

Good soil for the pond
● A clay and sand mixture in a ratio of 1:3 or 1:4, which is one part clay, three or four parts river sand (from a builders' yard, grains up to 2 mm in size).
● Special pond soil is also available, but do check the pH factor (see p. 41). If possible, the soil should not contain any fertilizer; if fertilizing becomes necessary, target individual plants; do not dose the entire soil (fertilizing, see p. 32).

● You will need to empty the water from the pond with a pump before putting in the soil layer. This should be at least 10 cm (4 in) thick, although it may be thicker in some places.

● First install the plants in this layer, then slowly fill the pond with water again.

Plant soil in an ornamental pond: If you are intending to keep fish in your pond, I recommend placing soil only in the marshy area. Any plants you set in the pond should be in baskets (see p. 35), then the water will remain clear even if you introduce fish that like to dig around at the bottom. A sand and clay mixture will be ideal for the marshy area and for the planting baskets.

● Mix aquarium soil (obtainable from aquarium suppliers) with builders' sand (sand containing clay) in a ratio of 1:3.

● Instead of builders' sand, you could use aquarium or birdcage sand (pet shop suppliers).

● A little crushed charcoal will offer protection against decay.

● This mixture will not tend to rise to the surface once it is under water. There is no need to weigh it down with gravel.

● Waterplant soil is special soil for ponds (obtainable in the gardening trade). Ask an expert at the garden centre what kind of fertilizer to use (the less, the better, see fertilizing, p. 32).

NB: The sand and clay mixture described above will be suitable for all plants which require soil containing lime. Never add peat to the planting soil!

Several kinds of marginal plants will have **special requirements** with respect to soil. If they require soil lacking lime (a peaty soil), add a little peat to the sand and clay mixture described above, using an average mixing ratio of 1:1:1, although for certain plants, like golden club

Water fringe (Nymphoides peltata) flowers all year round.

(*Orontium aquaticum*) and *Pontederia cordata*, the ratio should be 3:3:1.

Important: As peat may affect pond-water detrimentally, these plants should only be grown in a marshy area. They can be planted in latticed baskets together with other plants which require soil containing lime.

A choice of plants

The selection of possible garden-pond plants is so vast that they cannot all be described in this volume. Some of the most attractive plants are listed in the tables on pages 30-32. As the plants live in different depths of water in the wild, these requirements will have to be considered when choosing plants. When looking for plants for your pond, there are four basic types:

● marginal plants;
● surface plants;
● submerged, oxygenating plants;
● floating plants.

It is important for all areas of the pond to contain plants, which means that each of the four groups of plants should be represented as this is vital for the quality of the water and for the creatures that live in or around the pond (such as dragonflies or frogs).

NB: Only a few species are described for each of the four groups. Examples of further plants and special tips on care can be found in the tables on pages 30-32.

Marginal plants (for marshy areas): Only the roots and lower parts of the plants are submerged in water. They are planted in the shallow area of the pond, in a stream, in a marshy area or in very moist soil at the edge of the pond.

Amphibious bistort (Polygonum amphibium) flourishes both in marginal areas and in deeper water.

Surface plants: These plants root in the soil. Their leaves and flowers are set on long stalks and float on the surface of the water. In a garden pond they should be planted in areas that are deeper than 40 cm (16 in).

Submerged, oxygenating plants: These have leaves that remain underwater and only very exceptionally protrude above the surface. Many species root in the soil at the bottom of the pond but some float freely in the water. Most of them need plenty of light. Submerged plants should not be omitted in a garden pond as they are extremely important for the quality of the water: they produce lots of oxygen and also utilize waste products from fish, which, in turn, deprives algae of nutrients, helping to keep the growth of algae in check. Some species, like rigid hornwort (*Ceratophyllum demersum*), Canadian pondweed (*Elodea canadensis*) and water milfoil (*Myriophyllum*), grow very vigorously, so you should not plant too many of these species, to prevent the pond from becoming overgrown. In the case of smaller ponds, thin out the plants occasionally during the summer months.

Floating plants are plants with more or less defined roots, which float freely on the surface of the water. They can be installed in all areas of the pond. The only thing to watch out for is that the entire surface of the pond does not become overgrown, so install few plants and thin them out during the summer.

What to watch for when making a choice: Plants should be installed in all areas of the pond but make sure that at least a third of the surface is kept free.

● You will find details on the correct position and depth for individual species in the tables on pages 30-32.

● To begin with, do not employ too many plants or they will grow all over each other.

● Some marginal plants require soil that is poor in lime (peaty soil). Plan on placing these plants in a marshy area, not in the pond itself (see p. 22).

● Take note of the flowering time of the plants and choose plants to provide flowers from early spring through to the last warm days of autumn.

● Two, or even three, plants can be placed together in a basket. The plants should have the same requirements with respect to soil and position.

My tip: The following examples explain which plants can be planted together in a planting basket:

● common flag (*Iris pseudacorus*), bog bean (*Menyanthes trifoliata*) and water forget-me-not (*Myosotis palustris*);

● purple loosestrife (*Lythrum salicaria*), water mint (*Mentha aquatica*) and amphibious bistort (*Polygonum amphibium*);

● flowering rush (*Butomus umbellatus*), *Pontederia cordata* and water crowfoot (*Ranunuculus aquatilis*);

● branched bur-reed (*Sparganium erectum*), mare's tail (*Hippuris vulgaris*) and pond weed (*Potamogeton*).

Buying plants

Sometimes garden enthusiasts are gripped by a kind of madness when they go to choose plants for their garden ponds, being totally overcome by the range and the splendour of the colours. Usually, however, this can be resisted by the use of a pencil and paper. Make a planting plan and write down what is to grow where. This will take the pressure off your purse and your pond will not

Attractive marginal plants

These plants require soil containing lime (see p. 27).

Brooklime (*Veronica beccabunga*) For water up to depths of 15 cm (6 in), in a marshy area, or edge of a stream; blue flowers from late spring to early autumn. In the autumn, cut it back radically. It will not tolerate peat; if in a stream, place some limestones in the water.

Purple loosestrife (*Lythrum salicaria*) (see photos, inside front and back cover) For water up to depths of 15 cm (6 in), marginal zones, marshy areas and in streams. Flowers from mid-summer to the first month of autumn; blood-red inflorescences, usually more than 10 cm (4 in) tall. Do not place it with reeds or other fast-growing plants.

Water plantain (*Alisma plantago*) For shallow water (up to 15 cm or 6 in above the rootstock). Flowers from early summer to the middle of autumn; small flowers, white, rarely pink to reddish. In autumn, cut it back to just above the rootstock; after 1-2 years divide the rootstock and replant.

Monkey Flower (*Mimulus* species) For marginal areas of marshy ground. Flowers constantly from early summer until the first month of autumn; the flowers are various colours (yellow, pink, blue-violet).

Yellow loosestrife (*Lysimachia vulgaris*) For water of depths up to 5 cm (2 in); along the edges of streams. Flowers from early summer until late summer; the flowers are brilliant yellow. Tends to grow vigorously, so needs to be thinned out in summer and cut back in autumn.

Lobelia cardinalis For water of depths up to 15 cm (6 in), or in a marshy area. Flowers from late summer until mid-autumn; glowing red flowers. Do not allow it to become overgrown by other plants. If the pond is very unsheltered, overwinter the plants in a cellar.

Arrowhead (*Sagittaria sagittifolia*) For water of depths from 15-40 cm (6-16 in), edges of streams. Flowers from early summer until mid-summer; flowers white to reddish. Only the rootstock is hardy. Remove the remainder of the plant in the autumn. An important competitor with algae for nutrients!

Creeping-Jenny (*Lysimachia nummularia*) Will grow anywhere. Flowers from late spring until mid-summer; flowers yellow, about 1.5 cm (½ in). Easy to propagate; place a piece of stalk (with two leaves) in water and it will form roots.

Marsh marigold or **king cup** *Caltha palustris* (see photos, pp. 17 and 51) For water of depths up to 15 cm (6 in); marginal areas, marshy areas, stream edges (the roots must be in water). Golden yellow flowers from mid-spring until early summer. In shallow water, cut back four-fifths of the plant in the autumn. In other positions, leave withered foliage until spring.

Water forget-me-not (*Myosotis palustris*) Marshy areas, edges of streams. Flowers from late spring until early summer and from late summer until early autumn. Flowers are light blue to pale pink. In the autumn, cut back all parts of the plant protruding into the water to prevent decay and cut the other parts of the plant down to 5 cm (2 in) in the spring.

Mare's tail (*Hippuris vulgaris*) For water up to depths of 20-50 cm (8-20 in). Flowers from late spring to late summer. Will not tolerate peat; thin out regularly.

suffocate under masses of flourishing plants. Be warned, most garden pond plants tend to be quite small when they are bought! However, in a very short time they will develop into splendid plants which require plenty of room. If they do not have enough room to start with, they will become sickly and die.

Where to buy garden-pond plants

You can obtain plants for your garden pond in garden centres and nurseries. Healthy, disease-resistant water plants and marginal plants have been bred and raised by specialists over many generations of plants. These cultivars will grow and flourish in a garden pond without any problems.

Do not stock your pond with plants obtained from the wild, that is, from their natural habitats. The rarity and survival of water plants and marginal plants have become matters of great concern in the last few years on account of the draining and drying out of so many of the wetlands of Europe, and a safe future for the plants has only been secured in a very few areas. Many wild plants are now protected by law, so you could be breaking the law by removing them. Please also remember that every garden pond that has been properly installed and maintained is a small but active contribution towards nature conservation.

The following are *good sources* for purchasing plants, with selections large enough to meet all your wishes:

● aquarium suppliers and specialist garden centres;
● garden centres;
● specialist water garden nurseries which will often send plants by mail order;
● mail order firms.

My tip: Some water plant nurseries or garden centres have a selection of ready-made combinations of water plants, which they have put together for the initial planting of small ponds. When ordering these, all you need to do is give them the size of your garden pond and any special preferences you may have.

Tips on buying healthy plants

Take a careful look at the plants when you buy them or, in the case of mail order, when you open the package immediately it arrives. Healthy plants are identifiable by their roots.

● The roots must be white – bluish-black or brown root tips can indicate decaying plants.

● The rootstock, together with its "heart", which will later produce leaf shoots, should be large and healthy.

● Tubers or bulbs should feel firm.

● The rootstock should smell of fresh earth – on no account should it smell rotten. Exception: water lilies stink dreadfully as very often part of the rootstock has in fact died and decomposed. This is a completely normal state of affairs for water lilies and is in no way detrimental to their well-being.

My tip: If the plants are on sale in small plastic containers – which often happens nowadays – ask the salesperson to open the container so that you can take a good look at the roots.

Planting your purchases

When to plant: The best time to plant is during the growth phase when plants will be supplied with all the right conditions for growing well. This is during the period from mid-spring to early autumn. The careful gardener will always wait until the last cold snap of the last month of

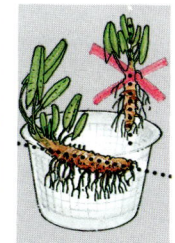

The correct way to plant water lilies
Remove all decayed parts and shorten the hair roots. Place the rhizome horizontally (not vertically!) in the basket. Carefully cover the rhizome with a sand and clay mixture (ratio 1:3). Gently press down the mixture. A layer of gravel is not absolutely necessary.

spring has definitely passed.
Important: Garden-pond plants should be planted as soon as possible after purchase, as storing them for a while is not good for them. If you cannot plant them immediately, you will have to water them well (container plants) or set them in a bath full of water. Dried-out pond plants are extremely difficult to revive.

Warning: Some water plants and marginal plants can prove harmful to human health, particularly if they are consumed by small children. If you are not an expert on plants, I recommend asking about this at the time of purchase.

Marginal plants with special soil requirements

These plants require soil that contains little lime; the best soil is a clay-sand-peat mixture (see p. 28). The most suitable ratio for this mixture should be indicated on a label tied to each plant.

Lysichithum americanum
For water up to 30 cm (12 in) deep. Brilliant yellow flowers from early spring to early summer. In regions with hard winters, over-winter plants in a cellar or somewhere similar; soil mixture 1:1:1.
Golden club (*Orontium aquaticum*)
For water up to 30 cm (12 in) deep; marshy area; needs sheltered position. Flowers from late spring to early summer. Flowers

brilliant yellow, protruding up to 10 cm (4 in) above the water's surface. In regions with harsh winters, overwinter the plant in frost-free conditions. Soil mixture 3:3:1.
Pontederia cordata (photo, p. 44) For water up to 20 cm (8 in) deep; marshy area. Flowers from mid-summer to early autumn; blue inflorescences. Proliferates vigorously; cut back radically in the autumn. Soil mixture 3:3:1.
Cotton grass (*Eriophorum* spp.) (photo, p. 45)
For the edges of marshy areas; very moist soil; should not stand in water. Flowers from late spring to late summer; seed heads are woolly, white. Soil mixture 1:1:1.

Surface and floating plants

In a small pond, which can also accommodate water lilies, vigorously proliferating floating plants should be installed sparingly. Make sure to thin them out often so that they do not take over the entire pond.

Pondweed (*Potamogeton* spp.) Surface plant. Grows anywhere in a pond. Flowers from late spring to late summer. Inconspicuous inflorescences. Thin out regularly; remove almost completely in the autumn. Competes with algae for nutrients; provides spawning places for fish.

Water fringe (*Nymphoides peltata syn Villarsia nymphoides*) Surface plant. For water up to 50 cm (20 in) deep. Brilliant yellow flowers from early summer to early autumn; flowers protrude a little above the water's surface. Remove nine-tenths of it in the autumn or the pond will become completely overgrown. Ideal environment for fish spawn and young fish.

Frog-bit (*Hydrocharis morsus-ranae*) Free-floating plant with surface rosettes. Will grow anywhere in the pond. White flowers from early summer to late summer. Cannot tolerate lime.

Water soldier (*Stratiotes aloides*) (see photos, p. 43 and back cover) Floating plant. Will grow anywhere in a pond. Flowers from early to late summer; white flowers with yellow anthers. Flourishes in nutrient-rich water, free of lime, but will cope with some lime.

Water lettuce (*Pistia stratiotes*) Floating plant. Will grow anywhere in a pond. No flowers. Leaves shaped like shells, set in rosettes.

Submerged, oxygenating plants

Although some of these underwater plants, like *Elodea, Ceratophyllum* (hornwort) and *Myriophyllum* (water milfoil), proliferate wildly and may fill up the pond, they should still be present (just do not plant too many!). They produce large quantities of oxygen and utilize the waste products of fish, which, in turn, deprives algae of nutrients. They are also ideal hiding places for young fish.

Water milfoil (*Myriophyllum* spp.) For water up to 50 cm (20 in) deep. Flowers from mid-summer to early autumn; pale pink inflorescence protrudes about 15 cm (6 in) above the water's surface. Water requirements depend on the water in which they naturally occur (ask at the garden centre etc.)

Rigid hornwort (*Ceratophyllum demersum*) Floats freely in the water. Does not flower. Forms tangles of plants that may be up to 1 m (40 in) across. Remove nine-tenths in the autumn. Will not cope with peat. Competes with algae for nutrients.

Duckweed (*Lemna minor*) Will grow anywhere in a pond. Does not flower. Fish out quantities of it regularly during the summer and remove nine-tenths in the autumn. Competes with algae for nutrients.

Canadian pondweed (*Elodea canadensis*) Grows anywhere in a pond. Rarely flowers in Europe. If lime is added to the water, it proliferates explosively! Remove nine-tenths in the autumn. Competes with algae for nutrients.

Preparing the plants

Before planting, a few measures are necessary, for example, cutting back the rootstock.

For these procedures you will need a sharp knife. Pruning clippers are not suitable as they squash and bruise the plants, which can lead to disintegration of the tissues and decay. The following points are very important:

● Remove all damaged or broken roots.

● Shorten long, straggling roots to a rounded ball.

● Carefully cut out decaying parts of the tuber or rootstock. Sprinkle a little charcoal powder on the cut surface to prevent decay.

● Remove damaged or bent leaves.

NB: Floating and submerged plants should be laid loosely in the water; marginal and surface plants should be planted in planting baskets, verge matting or in pockets in the same or directly into the soil.

Fertilizing

Many gardeners believe fertilizing will provide a good start for pond plants and will not harm them. My advice is that, apart from water lilies, you should not fertilize pond plants as fertilizer will merely support the formation of algae. Only add fertilizer to the soil in which water lilies are planted – they will then flower better. Use only a special aquarium or water plant fertilizer (and follow the instructions!). Ordinary plant fertilizers are no good as they may harm pondlife. In particular, they have a deleterious effect on the sensitive mucous membranes and respiratory organs of fish.

If you use ready-fertilized, water-plant soil, wait for two or three weeks before you put the fish in the pond, and change half of the water every week to eliminate any surplus fertilizer that is dissolved in the pondwater.

A glorious palette of colours for an ornamental pond.

Plants for an ornamental pond

1. *Nymphaea hybrid "Escarboucle"*, a splendid carmine red water lily with ruby red anthers and an orange yellow base. For a depth of 60-80 cm (24-32 in) of water.

2. *Nymphaea hybrid "Direktor Moore"*, a water lily with flowers that are 12 cm (4¾ in) across and large green pads. Must be overwintered in a frost-free position. For water 30-40 cm (12-16 in) deep.

3. *Nymphaea hybrid "Rosenymphe"*, a profusely flowering water lily with reddish-green leaves. The flowers turn white as they fade.

For water 30-70 cm (12-28 in) deep.

4. *Nymphaea hybrid "Moorei"*, a water lily with delicately scented flowers. For water 60-100 cm (24-40 in) deep.

5. *The yellow water lily (Nuphar lutea)* should be cared for in the same way as other water lilies. For water up to 40 cm (16 in) deep.

6. *Nymphaea hybrid "Laydekeri purpurata"*, a profusely flowering dwarf water lily whose foliage is brownish-red when it emerges from the water and then turns green on the surface. For water from 30-40 cm (12-16 in) deep.

7. *Iris sibirica hybrid*, one of the many colourful cultivars of the yellow iris. For water that is a maximum of 20 cm (8 in) deep.

8. The water hyacinth (*Eichhornia crassipes*) will only flower if the water temperature rises above 20°C (68°F). It will grow anywhere in the pond. Overwinter only in an aquarium.

9. Common flag (*Iris pseudacorus*), one of the most beautiful marginal plants, which only occurs rarely in the wild in a few areas (protected plant). For water up to 20 cm (8 in) deep.

Green and flowering garden-pond plants. The available selection is huge.

Plants for a nature pond or an ornamental pond

1. Branched bur-reed (Sparganium erectum), a hardy marginal plant which will also grow in deeper water. The seed capsules resemble hedgehogs in shape and appearance. For water up to 1 m (40 in) deep.

2. Hemp agrimony (Eupatorium cannabium), a vigorously growing plant for the moist marginal area. Thin it out occasionally during the summer.

3. Bog bean (Menyanthes trifoliata) will not tolerate lime; mix peat with the planting soil. Ideal for a marginal area or along a stream. Water up to 20 cm (8 in) deep.

4. Water crowfoot (Ranunculus aquatilis) is a toxic plant! It grows vigorously; thin out when necessary. A competitor with algae for nutrients. A good hiding place for small fry.

5. Flowering rush (Butomus umbellatus) should only be set in planting baskets in an ornamental pond as it has a widely spreading root system. For water up to 25 cm (10 in) deep; must always stand in water.

6. Water chestnut (Trapa natans) forms rosettes that float on the surface; turns red in the autumn. The mother plant will die off in the autumn; the fruits drop down and, in the spring, form new shoots.

7. Common bladderwort (Utricularia vulgaris), an underwater plant whose flowers protrude 15-20 cm (6-8 in) above the water's surface. The leaves are covered in numerous bladder-like tubes which serve to catch small water insects. Thrives best in water containing little lime and few nutrients.

Using planting baskets

If you do not want a real nature pond with a proper soil bottom which will manage for long periods of time without any special care, I can recommend placing your plants in planting baskets (see soil, p. 27). The growth of vigorously proliferating plants will be kept within bounds by these baskets and, in the autumn, when cutting back is required, they are easily lifted out of the pond (see p. 46).

Special lattice baskets for water plants can be obtained from the gardening trade in various sizes and shapes. Plants in baskets will receive an adequate supply of oxygen to their roots as the water moves gently through them.

My tip: Oval-shaped lattice baskets are ideal for the longish rootstocks (rhizomes) of water lilies.

Ordinary flowerpots are **unsuitable for waterplants**, as are plastic buckets with holes or PVC containers. The plant roots would not receive enough oxygen in these containers.

How to plant in lattice baskets

● Line the basket with a special thin planting material (obtainable in the gardening trade etc.) or with very thin foam rubber sheets (1-2 mm thick and decay-proof).
● Fill two-thirds of the basket with planting soil. Leave enough room so that the roots will not be bent upwards when the plant is inserted.
● The roots, tubers or rootstocks should be inserted in such a way that the tiny first shoots of the leaves point upwards.
Important: The rootstocks of water lilies must be laid horizontally in the soil (see illustration, p. 31).
● Now fill the rest of the basket with soil, making sure the shoots are still showing.

● Press the soil down gently and moisten it. The best idea is to stand it in a bath into which water can be poured very slowly, thereby moistening the soil from below.
● Covering the surface of the soil with gravel is not necessary if you use the soil recommended on page 27.

Placing the planting baskets in the pond

In the case of small ponds, the baskets can be put straight into the filled pond. If you do not wish to climb into the water in case the bottom will be churned up or because it is simply too cold, lay a beam across the pond and sink the baskets with the help of two long metal hooks.
Important: If you set the baskets in an empty pond, you cannot wait too long before letting in water, otherwise the plants will dry up. Fill the pond very slowly!
With the exception of water-lily baskets, all baskets can be placed in their final positions from the start. If you have an insulated pond, the baskets can be placed in the desired positions with the help of lattice bricks or stones which have been previously stuck to the insulation material with silicon adhesive.
Water-lily baskets should be moved several times as this will make the water lilies flower earlier and produce lots of blossom. Proceed in the following way with all water-lily baskets:
● In the spring, place the water-lily basket in shallow water.
● Lift the floating leaves up a little above the surface, then push the basket into deeper water until the leaves are barely submerged.
● Repeat the process, until the basket ends up in the desired position in deep water.

My tip: If, for some reason, you are unable to carry out this step-by-step procedure of gradually pushing the baskets into deep water, stack up as many roof tiles as possible in the desired final position to place the basket in a simulated shallow-water zone. Then lower the basket gradually, by taking away the tiles one at a time, until the basket is at the desired depth.

Verge matting

Verge matting made of natural fibres or plastic makes ideal plant containers for steep banks (see designing the edge, p. 22). Verge matting with integral planting pockets is the most practical form.

How to plant in the matting

● Anchor the matting with special fixtures, special nails or bolts intended for use in soil (obtainable in the gardening trade) beyond the edge of the insulation material at the edge of the pond.
● Fill the pockets with plant soil.
● Insert the plants from above through the mesh. The mesh can be pulled apart slightly to allow the roots to pass through without damaging them. Even plants with a compact rootstock can be planted in this way.

My tip: The verge matting should only be allowed to protrude a little way into the water of an ornamental pond. The interior of these mats will develop its own biological climate, which might create problems with algae in a pond stocked with fish.

Helpful gadgets

You cannot just let nature take its course in a small pond. In particular, ornamental ponds containing fish will need some care and equipment in order to meet the requirements of both fish and plants. Pondlife will only flourish without problems if you have the means to make sure there is a plentiful supply of oxygen and as little as possible in the way of waste products.

Technical devices

You will rarely need technical devices for a nature pond without a waterfall or stream. Life in such a pond is intended to develop and flourish undisturbed and to be self-regulating. In small nature ponds, however, there may be occasional disruptions, which will make the installation of an air pump necessary in order to supply the water with oxygen (see p. 39).
A water pump is indispensable if you wish a small waterfall or a stream to flow into your pond
An ornamental pond which is intended to provide a home for goldfish or koi and plants will hardly manage without some technological help. If you want to provide a healthy environment for your pondlife all year round, you will have to take control at certain times. Always keep two important points in mind:
● The pond requires an adequate supply of oxygen. It will be necessary to supply oxygen with the help of an air or water pump or with an oxygenator.
Important: The critical months, during which you will have to keep a sharp eye on the oxygen content of the water, are the last month of winter and the middle of the summer. Towards the end of winter, the water will begin to warm up slowly under the ice, while in the mid-summer months it is heated up far more than usual due to the weather. Both times may see a drop in the oxygen supply as warm water absorbs and stores less oxygen than cooler water.
● The pond must not be allowed to become overloaded with waste products, so a good filter will be necessary.

My tip: If possible, equip your pond with a stream of water. This will provide the best and most natural filter and oxygen provider (see p. 50). As long as the stream is flowing, you will not need technical gadgets for oxygenating or filtering.

Devices to aid overwintering (for example, ice-preventers combined with an oxygen supply) are important for both nature ponds and ornamental ponds. Even at times when a sheet of ice has formed on the surface, gases created through decay must still be able to exit through an ice-free spot in the pond, so that the overwintering pondlife is not harmed.
You will require a well-functioning *pump for running fountains* (see p. 25) or a stream (see p. 50) and for changing the water (p. 44).
The technical equipment needed for a garden pond is usually easy to run and all gadgets are obtainable through the gardening trade.

Accidents involving electrical equipment

Pumps and filters are run on electricity and everyone knows that electricity and water do not really mix, so, if the combination is handled carelessly, fatal accidents may occur. Safety must be made top priority during the installation of any electrical equipment or cables around or in a pond!
Take careful note of the following safety recommendations:
● Electrical installations should only be carried out by an expert!
● When you purchase equipment, make sure that it carries the British Standard kite mark (in the UK) or a similar guarantee of reliability in other countries.
● Use cables that are sufficiently long – never use extension leads!
● Turn off the power and always remove the plug from the socket before removing an electrical gadget from the pond!
● Repairs should only be carried out by an expert. If you carry out repairs yourself, or even make alterations to the device, you will be personally liable for any damage or accidents.
● Never remove a device from the pond by hauling it out by its cable.

My tip: Devices that are equipped with a handle or grip can be extracted from, or inserted into, the pond by means of a long piece of strong, bent wire or by a chain attached to the device, which is then anchored somewhere along the edge of the pond.

● A fail-safe switch will provide additional protection. If there is a

A small pond with red water lilies, water fringe and colourful flowering plants around the edge.

fault in the gadget or damage to the cable, the switch will immediately break the flow of the current. If you do not already have one, have a fail-safe switch built into your fuse box. If this is not possible, have the fail-safe switch inserted between the electrical source and the gadget.

Power supply
The routes of electrical lines running from the house or the position of electrical connections near the pond should be carefully considered when you plan your pond and should be installed during the pond-building phase.
Important: The best plan is to lay the cables through an underground PVC pipe (see p. 9). It is important to make sure that the underground cables will not be accidentally dug up by someone else in the garden or by any workmen who come to do

any form of work or repairs on your property. If you do not use a PVC pipe, use only rodent-resistant cables (specially designed for underground) and, again, never use extension leads! It is all too easy for extension leads to become disconnected, while rats and mice can cause unbelievable amounts of damage to wires and cables, making them both dangerous to use and expensive to replace.

Low-voltage electricity

Low-voltage (24 volt) electricity provides a high degree of protection against electric shocks or worse. Special water pumps and filters can be obtained in the gardening trade, which are designed for use with low-voltage electricity. In order to use these devices, you will need a low-voltage transformer which should be installed inside the house.

My tip: Lights installed in or around the pond (see p. 27) will run on 12 volts and can be run off a car battery.

Gadgets running on low-voltage electricity provide more protection but also use up more current than ordinary 240-volt equipment, as the transformer uses additional current. The transformer will often use as much current again as the pump itself.

Water pumps

You will need an electrical connection point for a water pump.

Use: Water pumps can be used for several different purposes.
● For agitating the water. By moving the water around, the pond is supplied with oxygen and a balance of temperature is attained between the sun-warmed upper levels of water and the colder, lower levels.
● For emptying the pond and for changing the water.
● For powering a running stream.
● For powering a waterfall or fountain etc.
● For filtering.

The right pump: There is a large selection of available pumps, so it is very important for a layperson to seek specialist advice (ask at your garden centre). Note the following points:

● Underwater or immersion pumps are the most useful and can be used for all the above-mentioned purposes. They are oil-cooled pumps that are hermetically sealed against water or set in artificial resin.
● They should be mounted on a lattice brick or fixed to a special pump mount in the pond.

Important: The pump should come supplied with proper instructions and state that it is suitable for operation under water. It should carry a relevant safety symbol (British Standard kite mark etc.).

Output of the pump: Pumps with an output of 360-2,000 litres per hour (79-440 gal per hour) should be quite sufficient for the above-mentioned purposes. The height of water moved (measured from the surface) can be up to 2 m (80 in). When buying the pump, indicate how you are intending to use it as a good salesperson will always give you the right advice.

My tip: Fountain pumps with a litre output of more than 10,000 litres (2,200 gal) per hour and able to move water 3 m (120 in) high are neither sensible nor necessary for a small garden pond. They are better for a fountain running in a separate basin (see p. 26).

Care of a pump: With regular servicing, a good underwater or immersion pump should run without problems for many years. Have your oil-cooled pump serviced by the manufacturer once a year (your retailer should take it in for servicing). If servicing is not carried out regularly, even the best pump can develop leaks around the seals so that oil escapes and pollutes the water. If the pump should run dry, only allow an expert to repair it! Pumps encased in artificial resin need practically no servicing.

Tips on use: To prevent plant debris from clogging the filter intake holes, the pump should not just be mounted on a lattice brick or fixed to a pump mount, but the intake holes should also be protected by an intake basket, a filter (filled with coarse nylon fibre waste), a plastic cage or a grid sieve (all obtainable from aquarium suppliers or in the garden trade).

Pumps not recommended: Air-cooled pumps should never be run under water. They should be installed in a frost-resistant pump shaft beside the pond. Some aquarium pumps, or even washing machine pumps, are totally unsuitable as they are not safe enough.

My tip: A solar pond pump is now available, which runs on solar energy with an output of 100 litres (22 gal) per hour under a clear sky. This is a new development which has probably not quite reached perfection yet but is definitely a step in the right direction.

Air pumps

If laying an electrical cable becomes necessary, the best

An oxygenator
An oxygen-providing device that will enrich water with oxygen all year round. It will continue to function during the winter, even under a covering of ice.

method is to lay an underground PVC pipe (see p. 9) and pull the electrical cable or the air line belonging to the air pump through it. The air line must be long enough to reach the deep-water zone if necessary. It should not be bent.

Use: These pumps provide a good service in both summer and winter.

● For supplying additional oxygen to the water: the pump blows air (and with it oxygen) into the pond and creates a revolution of the water at the same time to maintain the temperature balance between the water layers.

● For running a foam rubber or ceramic pot filter (see p. 40).

The right pump: You can choose between two types of pump:

● Ordinary air pumps are not resistant to splashes of water. They may only be suspended in a completely dry position (inside the house, or cellar), never outside.

● Splash-resistant air pumps (this must be stated in the instructions!) can be installed outside; this goes for garden pond air pumps too.

Tips on use: The ordinary pump must not be allowed to get damp, as it will then oxidize and this will cause it to become faulty. To prevent condensation (especially in winter) from running back towards the pump, it is worth installing a non-return valve (obtainable from aquarium suppliers or garden centres) between the pump and the stream stone (see column right). Please read thoroughly any instructions that come with a garden pond air pump as they will contain important information on setting it up and looking after it.

Impellers for an air pump

Impellers are connected to the air hose of the air pump to help with the oxygen supply and the movement of the water. Several different kinds of impeller can be obtained in

the gardening or aquarium trade.

Plastic and silicon dioxide impellers are cheap but rapidly become clogged up, so that they need to be cleaned and exchanged very often.

Ceramic impellers are a little more expensive than plastic and silicon dioxide ones, but more advantageous. They create a particularly fine "pearling" of the stream of air, which means an improved oxygen supply. They take much longer to become clogged. Impellers which have become clogged up can be baked over a gas flame (remove all plastic parts first!).

"Pearling" hose: This is a porous hose which can be connected to the air hose at any desired length. The fine pores create a kind of "oxygen curtain" which is particularly favourable for the circulation of the water. It will not clog up very quickly.

Oxygenators that are not run on electricity

These devices can be obtained in the garden trade under various names. They are particularly practical for gardens without a supply of electricity (like allotments).

Use: for additional oxygen supply in summer and winter. These devices will even function under a covering of ice.

How to use them: The oxygenator consists of a ceramic container with fine pores, which, in turn, contains a plastic container with a tiny catalyst. Some devices come equipped with several catalysts. (Do not lose the catalysts!) The device is filled with hydrogen peroxide. Read the instructions carefully!

Warning: Be careful when filling these! Hydrogen peroxide has corrosive properties. Store in a place

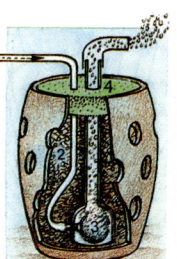

Garden pond filter
Left: ceramic pot filter.
Right: foam rubber filter.
Both gadgets are run on an air pump.

that is out of reach of children and animals!

Position: Stand the device in an easily accessible position in the pond.

Refilling: Hydrogen peroxide disintegrates to produce water and oxygen – the higher the temperature, the faster it will break down. When the contents are used up, the device will rise to the surface and will have to be refilled – in summer this will be approximately every six to eight weeks; in winter every three months.

Filters

A good filter is important in a garden pond stocked with fish as otherwise the water will become polluted with waste matter.

My tip: Use a special garden pond filter. Aquarium filters are too small.

Electric filter

Various types of garden pond filter can be obtained which are driven by a circulating pump.

Use: very easy to run, using very little electricity (from 10 watts). They can carry out several tasks at the same time in a pond:

A nature pond in autumn when the plants are preparing for winter.

- filtering;
- water circulation, during which the water is enriched with oxygen;
- running fountains or similar, for example, a small jet or water spout;
- ideal as a pre-filter (filled with small clay pipes) for powering a running stream.

Care: Apart from occasional cleaning out or changing the filter, these types of filters need practically no servicing.

Foam-rubber filters

The foam-rubber filter material will hold on to all kinds of debris, so the water is filtered mechanically. In addition, there is a small-scale biological filtering effect, as micro-bacteria colonize the pores of the foam rubber and, in time, break down organic debris.

Use: This filter is run on an air pump (see illustration, p. 39). It will keep 2 m^3 (71 ft^3) of pond water clean for one week (1 m^3 = 1,000 litres/220 gal). If you wish, several filters can be combined. Two filters will be quite sufficient for a pond that is about 6 sq m (64 sq ft) and contains about 3,000-4,000 litres of water (660-880 gal).

Care: Wash out the foam rubber once a week in lukewarm water (without any cleaners).

Ceramic pot filter

The filling material consists of lots of small clay pipes and foam rubber. It cleans the water mechanically, just like the foam rubber filter, and partly biologically too.

Use: It is run on an air pump, just like the foam rubber filter, and is used and handled in the same way.

Care: Wash out the pipes and the foam rubber in lukewarm water (no cleaners!) or fill with new clay pipes.

Winter dormancy; the pond will come to life again in spring.

Overwintering

During a hard winter it will often be necessary to make sure that there is an ice-free patch in the ice cover on your ornamental or nature pond (see p. 47). There are two practical devices to help with this.

An ice-preventer: which consists of special polystyrene parts (see illustration, p. 47). As it is not only very inexpensive but very simple to use (no electricity), I can highly recommend it as a reliable aid during the winter. The instructions are very easy to understand.

Pond heater: The name is rather misleading as the gadget does not actually heat the pond, but merely keeps a hole free of ice, at low wattage. You will need a supply of electricity. The device is switched on when the temperature drops below zero; when the thaw sets in, you can unplug it.

Important: Never use an aquarium heater with an extension cable in a pond!

My tip: If your pond heater should get frozen up because you have forgotten to put the plug in the socket, never try to hack it out with an ice pick. You would frighten the fish and, in addition, you might damage the cable, the cork float or even the heater itself, which might short-circuit the device.

How to care for your pond

During the summer, a pond does not create much work. Checking the water and looking after the plants does not take long. In the autumn, however, you should take some time to prepare the pond thoroughly for the approaching winter, so that fish and other pond creatures will survive the winter well and the plants will flower again the following spring.

Water

The degree to which plants and pond creatures feel at home in your pond will depend largely on the quality of the water. The decisive factors for this are the acidity (pH factor) and the nitrite and nitrate content. It is necessary to be aware of these values, so that you can intervene if it becomes necessary. For *ornamental ponds*, a regular check of the water is necessary so that, in an emergency, fast action can be taken.

In a nature pond which contains no, or few, fish, checking will only become necessary in the case of disturbances (like too much weed growth).

Measuring the water values

The pH factor and the nitrite and nitrate contents can be measured with simple, inexpensive procedures. The values obtained – the water values – will give you information as to whether intervention is required. Indicators (reagents), indicator strips and other agents can be obtained from the gardening trade. Exact, easy-to-understand instructions are supplied.

Acidity of the water

The degree of acidity of the water is expressed by the pH factor:

● a neutral reaction is indicated by a value of 7;

● values from 0 to 6.9 indicate that the water is acid;

● values from 7.1 to 14 indicate that the water is alkaline.

The right pH factor: pH values from 6.5 to 8.5 (slightly acid to slightly alkaline) are good for fish. Values below pH 6 may endanger your stock of fish.

The pH factor will fluctuate: During the course of a day, the pH factor may fluctuate slightly through the influence of the weather or through the presence of plants. These short-term fluctuations are normal and will not harm the fish.

Measuring the pH factor: During the warm part of the year you should make routine checks, with one measurement being particularly important:

● In the summer, after a heavy shower of rain, acid rain may detrimentally affect the pH factor.

● In the autumn, if leaf fall is heavy, large quantities of dead leaves may end up in the pond in a very short time. The rapid onset of decomposition may quickly reduce the pH factor to values around 5 – these are lethal values for most fish.
Regulating the pH factor: You will have to intervene if the pH factor deviates from values that are comfortable for fish.
● If the pH factor is too low: slowly change one-third of the water, and repeat if necessary.
● If the pH factor is too high: suspend a sack of garden peat in the pond until the desired value is attained. Check regularly as the pH value should not drop too low.

The nitrite and nitrate content
A constant process of change takes place in a pond. The organic waste produced by creatures and plants – for example, plant debris, excrement, remains of fish food – are decomposed by bacteria. This creates nitrites that are harmful to fish, which are then changed into nitrates which are harmless for fish. The process uses up oxygen in the water. As long as plenty of oxygen is available, and there is not too much waste matter in the water, this process will function without a hitch. The nitrite and nitrate contents will remain low and will not affect the well-being of the fish.
If the nitrite and nitrate contents become too high: The more waste matter that accumulates in the water, the greater the danger of nutrient over-enrichment and lack of oxygen. Too much nitrite is formed and also too much nitrate, which binds a lot of the oxygen in the water. The consequences are that:
● Too many nutrients lead to increased growth of algae.
● A high nitrite content will lead to symptoms of poisoning in fish.
● Due to a lack of oxygen, the fish

rise to the surface gasping for air (emergency respiration).
Prevention (important in an ornamental pond!)
For this reason, it is very necessary to:
● change one-third of the water every three weeks;
● feed the fish properly (see p. 57).
In an emergency: change the water and add an oxygenator (read the instructions carefully).

My tip: The best prevention is to employ a running stream as a biological filter (see p. 50).

Hardness of the water
The calcium and magnesium content of the water will determine the degree of hardness.
The various degrees of hardness of water are determined as follows:
5-10 degrees Clark = soft water;
10-21 degrees Clark = medium hard water;
22-38 degrees Clark = hard water.
Suitable hardness: medium hard, although many species of fish will cope with harder water. European mains water generally has the right degree of hardness. You can discover the degree of hardness of your mains water by approaching your local water authority or measuring it yourself with the relevant reagents.
Carbonate hardness is important for measuring water hardness. This indicates the amount of carbonates, which are compounds of calcium and magnesium with carbonic acid. The degree of carbonate hardness will determine how easy it will be to offset the fluctuations of the pH values, which would become extreme without the carbonate hardness and would have a lethal effect on many organisms. Carbonate hardness is part of the total hardness and is determined separately (reagents can be obtained from aquariums and aquarium suppliers).

The right water

Mains water is usually suitable for garden ponds. In some regions, however, mains water may contain a high amount of nitrates because residues from artificial fertilizers used in agriculture have seeped into the ground water. Later on, pond plants will absorb these products but there may be increased algae growth to begin with. In the case of water that is polluted with nitrates to a high degree, it is recommended that you add a suitable agent. (Ask at your garden centre.)

My tip: In some households, mains water runs through an ion-exchanger so that the pipes do not become furred up with calcium deposits. In this case, the water will have to be extracted from the mains before it reaches the ion-exchanger because the exchanger demineralizes the water, which may kill the fish.
Rainwater that has been collected outside can be used quite safely in your pond. If the rain runs through a roof gutter, however, you should wait for some time after long periods of dry weather, until the rain has washed away most of the accumulated dirt from the roof.

Exotic flowers and vivid green leaves
Water lilies, water soldier (Stratiotes aloides) and Pontederia cordata (in the background).

Filling and changing the water

As a rule, allow fresh water to run in very slowly. Connect a spray attachment to your hose. The fine spray will drive out any chlorine. Too much chlorine can lead to acid burns on the fishes' gills.

My tip: If you have one, check your water meter before and after the first filling of your pond. This will tell you the capacity of your pond. This value will dictate the number of fish you can install in the pond (see p. 55).

Emptying the pond: For this, you will need a water pump, to which you should attach a long hose. Make sure to equip the suction opening of the pump with a suction filter or it will become clogged with plant debris.

Changing the water in an ornamental pond: Change one-third of the water every three weeks, if possible. Add water treatment agents after the complete change of water following the autumn cut-back of plants (see p. 46).

Changing the water in a nature pond: Only do this in an emergency. If the water level has dropped sharply and no rain is expected within the forseeable future, allow water to run in very slowly.

What to do with the water from your pond

A huge quantity of water is involved in the changing of pondwater, certainly with a complete emptying and refilling. There are two ways of removing a large volume of water from a pond without too much fuss.

Allow it to soak away in the garden: If you use a water pump with an output of 1,000 litres (220 gal) per hour, the volume of water

Pontederia will require a soil consisting of a clay, sand and peat mixture.

moved when emptying a small pond (about 3,000-4,000 litres/660-880 gal) will soak away very easily in a normal, porous soil (lawn or flowerbed) without creating a flood. Watch the pond constantly during the removal of the water so that you can intervene if it does not soak away quickly enough. The water must not be allowed to penetrate your neighbours' gardens. Always allow the water to soak away a good bit before the boundary of your land. There should be no problems when removing only part of the water in your pond.

Using an outlet into the sewer: There is often the opportunity to conduct the water into the end of a downpipe from your roof gutter (house or garage). There is usually a water drain or gully at this point and sometimes you can push the hose into the downpipe or drain.

Responsibility for water damage

This is a very important point as far as you are concerned. If there is any damage, the conventional rule is that the person who built the pond and laid the water inlet or drainage line (whether this is the owner of the plot or a tenant) is the one who is liable. If a damaged water pipe or improper emptying of the pond leads to flooding of a neighbour's land, the responsible person pays the cost of the damage.

My tip: Check the water pipe regularly to make sure it is in order and, whenever you empty the pond, make sure no water is flowing on to a neighbour's land.

Cotton grass (Eriophorum), an ideal plant for the marginal area of the pond.

Controlling algae without the use of toxic substances

Algae do have a place in a pond. Without them the pond would be biologically dead. They fulfil important functions, such as supplying food for water snails and micro-organsims, and provide protection and a hiding place for fish. The algae should not, however, be allowed to gain the upperhand. The cause of excessive growth of algae is an accumulation of nutrients in the pond, caused by the decomposition of plants, animals, food and excrement as well as the addition of fertilizers.

Measures against excessive growth of algae

To keep algae growth within limits you must implement all of the measures mentioned below. One measure alone will not lead to success.

Plants: Employ marginal and water plants. They remove nutrients from the water, which will deprive the algae of their main source of food. Plants like *Elodea*, *Potamogeton* or *Myriophyllum* (water milfoil) should be included when stocking your pond but do not plant too many (see p. 29). As the growth of algae will increase with rising temperatures, shade-providing plants, like water lilies, *Nymphoides peltata* (water fringe) and other surface plants, will be useful aids in keeping the temperature of the water down.

Fish: Algae-eating fish, like grass carp (*Ctenopharyngodon idella*), silver carp (*Hypophthalmichthys molitrix*) and bitterling (*Rhodeus sericeus*), can be used to keep algae in check.

Water snails: If you introduce a few to your pond, they should not get out of hand as long as you do not feed the fish so much that remains of food sink to the bottom to provide extra food for the snails.

Care during the summer

The pond and pond plants will require only minimal care during the summer months; in the autumn, when you are making preparations for overwintering, more is involved in the way of care (see p. 46).

Ornamental ponds: Regular checks, changing water, routine checking of water values and a bit of care for the plants are all that is necessary.

Plants which proliferate vigorously will do so almost explosively in the spring, providing there are plenty of available nutrients. This may lead to the pond becoming overgrown, so that slow-growing plants, which do not flower until the autumn, are smothered. Another thing that may happen is that the nutrient supply required by the fast-growing plants is suddenly used up, which will make the plants die off rather rapidly. The debris will then decompose very quickly and this can often lead to a biological collapse of the pond within a few days. Fast-growing plants should, therefore, be thinned out regularly during the summer.

● Cut off troublsome growth as close as possible to the source with a pruning knife or rose clippers.

● Floating plants which have spread too widely can be fished out by hand or with a hand net.

Nature ponds: Only replenish water that has evaporated and, if necessary, thin out wildly proliferating plants. If the temperature of the water rises above 20°C (68°F), I urgently recommend supplying extra oxygen (see p. 39).

When building and caring for the pond, the following points should be borne in mind:

● Design your pond in such a way that remains of lawn fertilizer are not washed into the pond every time it rains.

● Routinely check the pH factor of the water and, if necessary, regulate it (see p. 42).

● Supply sufficient air. The more air that is pumped into the pond with an air pump, the more carbon dioxide is pushed out and the cooler the water will become.

● Carefully remove existing algae (long clumps and cotton wool-like formations).

● A running stream is recommended as a biological filter.

Unsuitable measures: I would strongly advise against employing chemical agents to control algae growth. These contain toxins that provide only temporary relief in removing algae, which will quickly grow back again.

Overwintering of the pond

When the temperature of the water falls below 12°C (54°F) in the autumn, the leaves will change colour and start falling and it is now time to carry out several measures to ensure that both fish and plants survive the winter safely.

Preparing an ornamental pond for winter

The most important signal for the start of autumn care is the temperature of the water. When it drops below 12°C (54°F), most fish will stop feeding.

Removing some of the pondwater: You will have to remove a good two-thirds of the pondwater before you can begin your preparations for the winter.

Catching the fish: As soon as the water has been removed, take out the fish and any amphibians (frogs and newts etc.). These creatures are easy to catch in shallow water with the help of a net or even with your hand if you are gentle.

Be careful: the sensitive mucous membranes of fish must not be injured. Immediately place the fish (not the amphibians, which would drown!) in a large, water-filled container (a bath or aquarium). The water should be provided with plenty of oxygen (use an air pump). Cover the container with a cloth as the fish might otherwise leap out because they have been scared by the catching procedure. Do not use a hard cover, which might injure the fish if they leap against it.

NB: Release the amphibians in a secure, damp, sheltered position near the pond.

Clearing out the pond: Decaying processes during the winter rest period might seriously lower the quality of the water. For this reason, everything that might decay during the winter should be removed from the pond.

● Stand all planting baskets by the edge of the pond. This will make it easier to work in the pond.

● The bottom sludge, which contains decomposed plant matter and other debris, should be completely removed if possible.

● The algae along the edge of the pond should be scrubbed off with a brush.

● Cut back all vigorously proliferating plants by four-fifths; they will start shooting again in the spring.

● Some plants (like water lilies), which have roots that grow as rhizomes, bulbs or tubers, will need special care.

● Please note the tips on care for individual species in the tables on pages 30-32.

Filling the pond again: After completing all the work, the pond can be filled with fresh water. The water should be treated with a suitable agent (obtainable from aquarium suppliers).

Preparing the pond for over-wintering

Change one-third of the water. The best way is to let the pond run over slowly. Only very large nature ponds, with a surface area of more than 50 sq m (537 sq ft) should be left without any preparation for the winter. In the case of a small nature pond, more care will be necessary otherwise it would silt up or even dry up within a few years' time.

Care of water lilies

The rhizome of the water lily is constantly growing at the tip and decaying somewhere else. It will, therefore, always smell rather strongly of rotten eggs. When the water lily root is submerged in the pond, however, you cannot smell it and it does not affect the beauty or health of the plant.

Care: Water lilies (and all other plants with rhizomes) must be transplanted in the autumn.

● Cut back the rhizome by a third and remove all decaying parts with a sharp knife.

● Remove leaves, flowers and stalks. Do not cut off any embryonic leaves or flowers that are already present in autumn. The young leaves are rolled up and shaped like arrowheads.

● Plant the rhizome again, in a larger planting basket if necessary.

● Hardy species can be planted in the deepest part of the pond.

● More sensitive species should be overwintered in a frost-free position, covered with dead leaves, preferably in a cool cellar. Check the rootstocks occasionally, as decaying parts should be removed.

Propagating: Water lilies are easy to propagate in the autumn. Divide the rhizome between the buds (where shoots will grow) with a sharp knife. The buds are shield-shaped, usually triangular, and about the size of a fingernail. Set the divided rhizome pieces in planting baskets.

Care of bulbous or tuber-like roots

The bulbous or tuber-like swellings of the root system must not be damaged as the rootstock would then quickly decay and the plant will die.

Care: In the case of perennials, remove only the leaves in the autumn, then carefully remove the

After preparing the pond and the other plants, place the baskets of water lilies in the deepest part of the pond and insert a device for keeping a hole in the ice.

Covering the pond
Lay the air pump hose in a medium-deep part of the pond. Stand a lattice brick at the northern edge of the pond. Arrange wooden rafters in a grid pattern and lay a transparent corrugated plastic sheet over them.

young tubers and set them in a planting basket. In the case of annuals, like *Sagittaria sagittifolia* (arrowhead), the mother plant, which dies in the autumn, is removed and the young tubers are planted.

Overwintering fish in a pond

If your fish are to overwinter in a pond, measures must be taken to ensure that the fish survive the winter safely. Even if you were to adopt only one of the measures described below, this would benefit the fish and the entire pond. The best results will be obtained, however, if you combine several of the measures or even use all of them.
NB: All overwintering measures will also benefit pond visitors that overwinter in the water (such as dragonfly larvae, snails and frogs).
Warning: If the deep-water zone is less than 70 cm (28 in) deep, you should overwinter the fish in an aquarium. In order to find out how to do this, you must consult a book on aquariums or seek advice from an aquarium expert.

Covering the pond

In my experience, the ideal overwintering measure is to cover the pond with transparent material. This will help to utilize the sun's warmth, just as in a cold frame or greenhouse.
The time for covering up is before the leaves begin to fall from the trees. This will prevent the wind from depositing large quantities of leaves in the pond.
Covering material: glass, plexiglass or corrugated plastic. Corrugated, transparent plastic is very stable and tough and can be rolled up when not in use (saving storage space during the summer). It can be obtained from builders'

merchants in various widths (up to 4.5 m or 15 ft).
Method (see illustration left)
● Place the covering over the pond at an angle so that rainwater will run off the upperside and condensation can run off the underside, and so that a slight but vital amount of ventilation is assured.
● The slope of the covering should face south.
● Weigh down the edges of the covering with lattice bricks.
● In regions that experience frequent falls of slushy snow, support widths of corrugated plastic that are longer than 2.5 m (8 ft 4 in) with lengths of wood (24 x 48 mm or 1 x 2 in). Arrange the lengths of wood like a grid, spacing them 60-80 cm (24-32 in) apart.
Care: Sweep off thick layers of wet, slushy snow. Powdery snow can be left, as it is an excellent additional insulator which will considerably hinder ice formation on top of the pond.

Keeping a hole free of ice

If you can keep part of the surface of the pond free of ice all winter, by using a pond heater or ice-preventer, you will ensure an adequate supply of oxygen. How these devices operate is described on page 41.

An oxygen supply during the winter

If you have a covered pond containing few fish, you need not necessarily add oxygen (although it is better if you do). However, you will have to provide additional oxygen if:
● a covered pond is stocked with lots of overwintering fish;
● the pond is not covered.
Air pump: Blowing in air will provide the pond with necessary oxygen and will hinder constant freezing up.

● Lay the air hose in a medium deep part of the pond. If air is blown in at the deepest part, a rather strong current would be created in the pond. This would be stressful for the fish and they would tend to lose condition.

My tip: Hang the air pump up in a heated room so that warmer air is pumped into the pond. Again, this will hinder rapid freezing over of the pond.

Oxygenator: This can provide up to three months' supply of oxygen under the ice, but it will not keep a hole open in the ice as an air pump will.

What you should not do!

Never hammer a hole in the ice cover. You will only succeed in disturbing the dormancy of fish and other pond creatures. It would probably frighten them so much that they would start swimming around in a panic and might injure themselves badly. Never throw polystyrene, twigs, bundles of straw or car tyres into the pond to prevent freezing up. This would do more harm than good.

Pond care in the spring

If you have prepared your pond properly for the winter, just a few measures will be necessary in spring to prepare it for the summer.
● Check the reinforcement of the banks and secure loose stones or pavingstones.
● Check the drainage (soak-away, see p. 18) and make sure it is not clogged with decomposing leaves.
● Check all gadgets to make sure they are functioning properly.
● Resume use of the filter or stream (see p. 50).
● Lower the water lilies gradually, at intervals of one week (see p. 35).
● Test the water and, if necessary, regulate (see p. 42).
● In the first month of spring, add plants if required.
● Once the temperature of the water rises above 10°C (50°F), start feeding the fish that have overwintered in the pond.
● Do not put fish that overwintered in an aquarium back into the pond until the difference in temperature between the aquarium and the pondwater is only a few degrees. Reintroduce the fish into shallow water!
Problems can appear in spring if you neglected to care for the pond in the autumn. It is quite likely that not all of the pondlife will have survived if your pond was not properly prepared for winter. If you have been negligent, by early spring the oxygen content of the water will be so low that you really must take measures, during the last month of winter and in early spring, to prevent the biological collapse of the pond and damage to the fish.

Danger signal! You must act quickly if the fish come up to the surface to gasp for air as they may end up freezing to the still existing ice cover. Take the following action:

● Immediately blow in oxygen and thaw the ice at the relevant place with a stream of water.
● Let fresh water into the pond very slowly!
● Remove the ice cover. It will be lifted up by the rising water level, so it can easily be broken and lifted off.
● Afterwards, let more water run in and, by allowing the pond to run over, gradually exchange the water in the pond.
● Fish out any sludge that rises to the surface, using a net.
● On no account feed the fish, even if they are swimming around at the top. As soon as the oxygen situation has normalized, they will return to the deeper regions of the pond until the temperature of the water rises.

How to indentify and control problems

Symptoms	Possible causes	Remedy
The water is transparent but amber-coloured. New leaves of plants are slightly reddish (for example, the submerged leaves of arrowhead).	The nitrite and nitrate contents are too high; the pH value is too low, probably below 6; too much humic acid caused by too much peat; large quantities of dead leaves in the water.	Slow change of water; for three days running, change one-third of the water; check the nitrite and nitrate contents and the pH factor; if the nitrite content is too high, use a water-improving agent. Remove peat and dead leaves.
The water is transparent but amber-coloured, rising bubbles do not burst immediately at the surface. If oxygen is added, foam forms. The fish are swimming at the surface, gasping for air and "swaying". The plants are losing leaves, the water lilies are no longer flowering properly.	The pond is overloaded with harmful substances; dying plants, algae and excrement are being broken down by bacteria as not enough movement is taking place in the deeper levels of the water; oxygen-poor deep-water zone where the plants are short of oxygen around their roots.	Vigorous airing is required (air pump); thin out plants; remove algae; change one-third of the water; fish out decomposed leaf remains lying on the surface using a wide-mesh net.
The water is the colour of white coffee; all levels of the water are cloudy. The plants are growing well. The goldfish are well, but all other fish are dying.	Too many carp-like fish churning the bottom up because they are getting too much food; the carbon dioxide content of the water is too high (oxygen for fish is sufficient). Possibly, sand or humus has got into the pond.	Clean out filters and the course of a stream; almost complete change of water; vigorous airing to get rid of excessive carbon dioxide; employ an oxygenator.
The water is bright green. The plants are growing well. The fish are thriving.	Explosive proliferation of *Volvox* spp. (a single-cell organism containing chlorophyll).	Silver carp eat *Volvox*, or employ an oxygenator. Introduce fresh-water mussels. *NB:* Chemical water-cleaning agents may cause biological collapse.
The water is clear in the morning, but becomes milky and cloudy towards the evening in the upper levels. The plants are thriving. The fish are having trouble breathing, swim close to the surface and gasp for air.	Explosive proliferation of micro-organisms.	Do not change the water; vigorous airing required. In minor cases, lowering the pH factor with peat may help, otherwise use a chemical water-cleaning agent (follow the instructions meticulously). *Warning:* These agents are toxic. Store them in a safe place as they must be kept away from children and pets!

The stream – a biological filter

The best and most natural filter for a pond is a slow-flowing stream which rises near the pond or somewhere in the vicinity and then runs into the pond. It also creates additional habitats for many green and flowering plants and numerous animals. Even if you have only a small pond, it is no great problem to install a stream to provide clean water for the pond.

The functions of a stream

As a biological filter: A stream that has been properly designed and constructed, with plenty of plants on its banks, has a cleansing effect on an ornamental or nature pond and improves the living conditions for animals and plants. Waste particles are captured in it, and the bacteria living in the stream break down such organic waste into nutrients that can be used immediately by plants. When the stream is full of running water, from spring to autumn, it will admirably fulfil its purpose as a biological filter.

As a habitat, it is a magnet for many animals. Frogs, toads, newts, dragonflies and butterflies will find plenty of food in and around the stream, along with suitable places for breeding. As these visitors would find it hard to survive over long periods of time in an ornamental pond stocked with goldfish, the stream is a good way to invite them to make a home in your garden.

Planning the course of the stream

The course of a stream will have to be planned and built just as carefully as a pond if it is to fulfil its function.
Calculating the length of the stream: The stream must be of a certain length in order to act as a biological filter. The required length will depend on the volume of water in your pond.

General rule

When calculating the length of the stream, estimate 1.5 m (5 ft) per cubic metre (1,000 litres or 220 gal) of water. A pond with a surface measuring 6 sq m (64 sq ft) will contain approximately 4 m³ (4,000 litres or 880 gal) of water, so the stream should be 6 m (20 ft) long.
The width and depth of the stream: The best measuring device is your spade. The bed of the stream should be one spade's depth (about 25 cm or 10 in) and two spades' width (about 50 cm or 20 in).
Course: Do not be perturbed by the required length of the stream. In most gardens a stream measuring 6 m (20 ft) in length (or longer) is easy to accommodate. For example, you can lead the stream right around the pond, along a fence or in S-bends around trees. Work out the future course of the stream by laying out a long garden hose.
Insulating materials: there are several possibilities.
● PVC pond lining is excellent.
● Ready-made parts, made of fibreglass or natural sandstone, or basin-like shapes, which are basins linked together to form a stream.
● I would advise against all other materials, like clay or concrete, as they create far too much work.
The gradient: If you use PVC pond lining material or pre-moulded basins, you will have to provide a gradient (see p. 51). The natural sandstone basins can be slotted into each other in such a way that they create a gradient.

How to build the course

The following instructions apply to the building of a stream using PVC lining material. The information given here is also applicable to artificial basins.

A stream with king cups (marsh marigolds) and a mass of Primula.

Constructing a gradient

The gradient is very important when laying the bed of the stream as the water is pumped from the pond into the beginning of the stream and will have to flow slowly downhill, along the course of the stream, and back into the pond without any additional means of power supply.

The right gradient: A gradient of 25 cm (10 in) for a distance of 3 m (10 ft) or 50 cm (20 in) for a length of 6 m (20 ft) is quite adequate. If the water is intended to flow into the pond via a small waterfall (see p. 52), raise the beginning of the stream further, so that there is enough gradient at the end of the route to create a waterfall.

Earthworks: Before you begin to move any earth, you should lay out the course of the stream using a rope and some small wooden pegs.

● In most gardens, the only way to create the necessary gradient is to build a mound. The earth you have dug out for building the pond is ideal for this purpose.

● If a natural gradient already exists (if your garden is on a slope), digging a trench along the course will direct the flow of the stream.

Building the bed of the stream: On the mound or slope, dig the bed of the stream to one spade's depth.

Installing a waterfall: My advice is to install a small waterfall at the mouth of the stream. The enormous quantities of bacteria that will colonize the stream and perform valuable filtering services, will also create a surplus of carbon dioxide in the water.

If this water, now saturated with carbon dioxide, were allowed to flow back into the pond, it would lead to excessive growth of algae. A small waterfall installed at the end of the stream will drive out any surplus carbon dioxide and supply the water with oxygen.

My tip: If you really do not want a waterfall, lay a few stones the size of tennis balls in the stream; they will provide plenty of turbulence so that enough oxygen is mixed with the water.

Securing the banks: This is advisable, particularly if the subsoil is fairly soft and at bends in the stream where the soil will tend to be washed away. You can build a bank with the earth dug out of the stream bed. The banks can be secured with:
● stones;
● large boulders;
● vertically buried lengths of rounded wood.

How to insulate the stream with PVC lining
The lining should be laid in the same way as described for the pond.
Measuring the lining material: Again, the best aid is your garden hose.
● Measure the width by first laying

Building the course of a stream
Line the bed with PVC pond liner. Reinforce the banks with stones. Fill the bed with filling material (gravel). Lay a few stones (the size of tennis balls) in the bed of the stream.

the hose across the stream bed.
● Measure the piece of hose with a measuring tape.
● Very important: add 30 cm (12 in) of lining material along the edges on both sides, just as you did for the pond.
● Now measure the length of the stream with the help of your hose. Add another metre (40 in) at the end, so that you may be sure the length of lining material will be sufficient.
Joining the lengths of lining material: If you are prepared to add a little to the cost of purchase, you may be able to leave the joining of the lengths of PVC lining to the manufacturer. If you wish to do it yourself, make sure, when it comes to welding the lengths together, that you follow the instructions meticulously, especially any recommended safety precautions (see p. 13).
Joining the lining of the stream bed to the pond lining material: At the mouth of the stream, the stream lining will have to be joined to the pond lining with great care. No water should be allowed to leak away as this would cause the pond to lose considerable amounts of water. There is no need to do any joining at the beginning of the stream's course.

Filling material and reinforcing the banks
Before securing the lining material at the edges of the stream, you must install the filling material on the bed of the stream. This is the first step towards turning the stream into a filter. The filling material provides the same function as a mechanical filter by trapping particles of debris as they are carried downstream by the water. This additional biological effect of the stream should have begun about a fortnight after the stream begins to flow. Bacteria colonize the filling

Placing plants in the stream
Set the plants in narrow, rectangular baskets. Bury them in the gravel, alternating them, as close to the bank as possible.

material and then break down the trapped organic debris in such a way that it can be used as nutrients by the plants.
Suitable filling materials:
● gravel (grains of 5-7 mm);
● quartz pebbles.
Warning: Do not use limestone gravel. If water runs through limestone gravel, this may, in the long run, have a detrimental effect on the pH factor by driving it up too high.
Sources: You can obtain cleaned filling material in the gardening trade, which can be used right away. If you buy material from builders' merchants, you will have to wash it yourself before use.
Quantity: You will need about 25 kg (55 lb) of filling material per metre of the stream's length. The stream bed is filled up in such a way that the top edges of planting baskets will later be submerged in the filling material.
Trial run: Before burying the lining material at the edges of the stream, do a trial run by letting water run down the stream.
● With the help of a pump and a connecting hose, run water into the stream.
● Observe the rate of flow. The stream should flow slowly. If it flows too fast, it will lose part of the filtering effect.
● By making the bed of the stream

deeper, you can speed up the flow; by making the bed more shallow, you can slow it down.

● Now is the time to make any necessary corrections to the edges of the stream.

Fixing the lining material to the edges of the stream: There must be no capillary action along the edges of the stream (see p. 14). The lining material should be laid over the stones or rounded wood sections used for securing the banks, then buried along the edge so that the ends of the material are pointing upwards. You can place plants along the edges of the stream or let a lawn grow over them.

Installation of a water pump

The water supply of the stream is ensured by means of a water pump.
Position: It should be set up as far as possible from the pond end of the stream. The length of hose from the pump to the beginning of the stream should be as short as possible. If the pump were to be situated too close to the mouth of the stream, it would suck in the already-filtered stream water and very little of the dirty pondwater would end up in the stream.

The output of the pump: The stream should flow very slowly. The faster it flows, the less filtering will take place. For this reason, stream pumps with an output of between 360 litres (79 gal) at 6 watts and 200 litres (44 gal) at 19 watts are quite sufficient (see p. 38). The low-voltage pumps described on page 38 are also very suitable for powering the stream.

Unsuitable pumps: With their huge output, fountain pumps would churn the stream up so much that the filtering effect would be lost and the filling material would be washed into the stream. The stream would also rise and overflow, so that the pond would soon be empty.

Plants along the stream

The stream would not be complete as a biological filter if there were no plants in it. The substances broken down by bacteria in the water have to be utilized by plants in the stream, otherwise there would be an excess of nutrients in the pond, which would create an increased growth of algae. If your stream is to be a perfect biological filter, you cannot be stingy with plants.

Suitable plants: Many attractive marginal plants are suitable for a stream too. Choose fast-growing, medium-tall plants that can tolerate regular cutting back of leaves near the roots. Suitable stream plants are water crowfoot, irises, cotton grass, lemon balm, water mint, forget-me-not, dwarf bulrushes, rushes, sedges, branched bur-reed, creeping-Jenny and arrowhead (see plant tables, pp. 30-32).

Planting: Good planting soil is provided by a soil mixture that is poor in nutrients (sand and clay in equal parts).

● Set the plants in narrow, rectangular planting baskets (obtainable in garden centres).

● Sink the baskets into the filling material in the stream as close to the banks as possible and alternate them, so that two baskets are never opposite each other.

This arrangement will ensure that the water does not flow straight down the middle of the stream but has to meander around each basket, which extends its path and slows down the rate of flow.

Plants for your stream

Brooklime (*Veronica beccabunga*) 20-30 cm (8-12 in) tall, prostrate growth. Blue flowers from late spring until early autumn.

Purple loosestrife (*Lythrum salicaria*) (see photos, inside front cover and back cover)
Up to 1.20 m (48 in) tall, flowers from mid-summer until early autumn, blood red, usually over 10 cm (4 in) long.

Yellow loosestrife (*Lysimachia vulgaris*)
Up to 1.5 metres (5 ft) tall. Brilliant yellow flowers from early until late summer. Thin out in the summer; cut back radically in the autumn.

Sweet flag (*Acorus calamus*)
Up to 80 cm (32 in) tall. Only flowers occasionally in temperate climates, from early to mid-summer. Flowers small and greenish.

Arrowhead (*Sagittaria sagittifolia*) Arrow-shaped leaves. Flowers from early to mid-summer, rarely later; white to reddish on a robust stalk. Only the bulb-like root clump overwinters, the rest of the plant dies (remove in the autumn).

Marsh marigold or king cup (*Caltha palustris*) (see photos pp. 17 and 51)
Forms cushions that are usually 20 cm (8 in), rarely 50 cm (20 in) tall. Yellow flowers from mid-spring to early summer. Important: do not remove the dead foliage until the spring.

Water mint (*Mentha aquatica*)
Grows up to 60 cm (24 in) above the surface of the water; the 3-cm (2 in) leaves smell of peppermint when rubbed. Lilac to violet flowers from mid- to late summer. Remove the plants as far as possible in the autumn.

Overwintering the stream

In summer the stream will require no special care. If necessary, you can thin out the plants occasionally if they proliferate too much.

My tip: During the warmer part of the year, if possible, do not ever switch off the pump that runs the stream, or, if you do, not for any length of time as the stream would then no longer function well as a biological filter. In as short a time as two or three hours, the bacteria would die through lack of oxygen.

In the autumn, when you are preparing your pond for winter, the stream should be turned off.
● Turn off the pump and remove it from the pond.
● Cut back the plants and thin them out.
● Place the fish in the pond or in a cold-water aquarium.
Early in spring, clean the stream out before starting it again, as decaying matter will have accumulated on the bottom during the course of the winter.
● Rinse the filling material on the bottom of the stream bed with a vigorous stream of water from a hose.
● After cleaning the stream, pump one-third of the water out of the pond and then allow fresh water to run in slowly. This means that a large amount of the dirty, cloudy water will immediately be removed from the pond.
● Connect up the stream pump and pump water into the stream.
● If necessary, change another third of the pondwater.

An ornamental pond with goldfish
A pond like this is an ideal environment for the most popular pondfish, the goldfish, which can be obtained in many colourful varieties.

Fish and other inhabitants of a garden pond

Gleaming goldfish, colourful koi or less-exotic native fish will bring life to your pond. With the right selection of fish and proper food and care, you should have many years' pleasure from your fish. Furthermore, if you are able to provide the right habitat for them, a few visitors may also turn up and even make themselves at home, like frogs, newts, toads, dragonflies, butterflies and other fascinating creatures.

Tips on buying fish

The best place to buy fish for your garden pond is at an aquarium supplier.
Goldfish and koi, the most popular garden-pond fish, are regularly for sale in garden centres or aquarium suppliers, or they may be able to obtain them for you.
Other fish, like *Leucaspius delineatus* or *Phoxinus phoxinus* (minnow), are more difficult to get hold of. Ask your local aquarium supplier if he or she can find you healthy, suitable fish. Never go to catch fish in the wild. Many indigenous fish are protected by law. Furthermore, wild specimens usually have a hard time getting used to conditions in a garden pond.
Some basic points to watch out for when buying fish:
● Find out first about the requirements of the fish you wish to keep (ask an aquarium supplier or consult a good book on keeping freshwater fish).
● If other pond owners offer you fish, do not just look at the fish but also take a look at the pond where they live – the symptoms of a "sick pond" can be found on page 49.
● Fish for consumption and bait fish do not belong in a garden pond. Fish used for bait are usually infested with disease.

Tips on choosing fish

The number, size and lifestyle of the fish will be important factors when you are choosing fish, particularly if you are putting together a community of different species.

How many fish to have?
You will find tables of recommended fish stocks on page 57. These communities of fish should thrive in a well-cared-for ornamental pond. You should, however, restrict yourself to only a few fish in a nature pond.

Fascinating fish which will feel right at home in a well-cared-for garden pond.

Fish for your garden pond

1. Three-spined stickleback
(Gasterosteus aculeatus). The male's underside turns brilliant red (see photo) at spawning time. This fish has three spines which it can raise in front of its dorsal fin. Predatory, so do not introduce more than two couples to your pond. Acclimatizing is a little difficult for this species. Will eat anything it can swallow!

2. Goldfish (Carassius auratus). The most popular of all pond fish. There are many breeding varieties, which differ in colour and the shape of their bodies and fins. Keep them as a shoal. Excellent biological filtering is necessary. Omnivorous, will eat animals or plants, and like commercial fishfood. Reproduction is problem-free in a garden pond.

3. Minnow (Phoxinus phoxinus). The male displays a red belly and edges to its lips during spawning time (see photo). Keep as a shoal. Very suitable for small ponds. Eats insects, their larvae and small crustaceans. Protected species in the wild!

4. Leucaspius delineatus. Keep in small shoals. Does not like water containing lime. Eats insects, their larvae, small crustaceans, submerged algae.

5. Golden orfe, a variety bred from the orfe (Leuciscus idus). Keep in a small shoal. Good insect eater. Eats everything, mainly flying insects (crane flies).

6. Bitterling (Rhodeus sericeus). Introduce at least four to six specimens. Eats insect larvae (mosquito and midge larvae), likes commercial fishfood. Needs freshwater shellfish for its reproductive cycle. The wild European species are protected.

The lifestyles of fish

Fish are divided into two groups, depending on their habits – predatory and non-predatory fish. Both groups can live together in one pond, but in a small pond you will have to keep an eye on the numbers of fish and maintain the correct ratio (see tables right).

Predatory fish: Introduce them only in pairs (and keep only a few pairs).

Non-predatory fish: introduce a small shoal. The shoal will provide protection against enemies. Only if a fish is too slow or too sick to swim with the shoal will it fall prey to the predatory fish.

Shoals of fish in a garden pond

Introduce at least ten specimens of one species. For example, if you introduce too few orfe, they will remain shy and stay in the deeper water all the time. If you want lots of different species of fish, you should restrict yourself to one shoal of orfe and introduce only a few other species.

Leucaspius delineatus and rudd (*Scardinius erythrophthalmus*) will feel quite comfortable in a shoal of orfe; koi (Japanese carp) will enjoy swimming with a shoal too (see table right, non-predatory fish).

Useful fish

When choosing fish you should not forget those species that are extremely useful in a pond on account of their food intake.

Algae eaters: Algae-eating fish will keep the growth of algae in your pond in check. I know of three different algae-eating species, each of which specializes by eating different types of algae:

● the grass carp (*Ctenopharyngodon idella*) eats all species of filamentous algae;

● the silver carp (*Hypophthalmichthys molitrix*) eats submerged algae;

● the bitterling (*Rhodeus sericeus*) eats blue algae.

NB: If, temporarily, there is not enough algae in the pond to satisfy these fish, they will also eat commercially produced fish food.

Insect eaters: Insects are an important source of food for some fish, which keeps the numbers of insects in and around the pond in check.

● Golden orfe live mainly on flying insects. Their favourite food is mosquitos and crane flies.

● Gudgeon (*Gobio gobio*) eat dragonfly larvae and diving beetle larvae.

● *Leucaspius delineatus* lives on flying insects and particles of algae.

Feeding fish

Feeding the fish is just as much fun for adults as it is for children but you can quickly overdo things. Incorrect feeding may lead to disturbances in the natural balance of the pond, so you should observe several important rules and also explain to your children how to feed the fish correctly.

Suitable food: Commercially produced fish food (flakes or feeding sticks), which is specially prepared for garden-pond fish, can be obtained from aquarium suppliers. Species of fish which prefer animal food can be offered live food occasionally. This can be fresh, freeze-dried or deep frozen, and is also obtainable from aquarium suppliers.

Harmful food: stale bread and kitchen refuse of any kind. If you give the fish live food, do not give them *Tubifex* spp. (worms) as they are carriers of dangerous diseases.

Fish stocks
Non-predatory and predatory fish

Size of pond: 6 sq m (64 sq ft)

Species	Number	Details
golden orfe	10	non-predatory, insect eater;
stickleback	4	predatory, territorial;
grass carp	3	non-predatory, algae eater;
gudgeon	2	predatory;
bitterling	4	non-predatory, tends young;
Leucaspius delineatus	5	non-predatory, insect and algae eater;
pumpkinseed fish	8	predatory, interesting mating habits.

Fish stocks
Non-predatory fish

Size of pond: 6 sq m (64 sq ft)

Species	Number	Details
golden orfe	20	insect eater (flying insects);
grass carp	4	algae eater (filamentous algae);
silver carp	2	algae eater (submerged algae);
goldfish	4	no problems reproducing;
gudgeon	2	eats dragonfly larvae and larvae of diving beetles;
bitterling	4	interesting care of young;
koi	3	colourful ornamental fish.

A properly built and well-established garden pond offers food and shelter to many other animals.

Visitors in and around a garden pond

*1. **Dragonfly** larvae live entirely in water during their very long period of development. When they emerge to metamorphose, the nymphs crawl up the stem of a plant and unfold their wings as splendid dragonflies.*

*2. **Great diving beetle** (Dytiscus marginalis). A diving beetle which can also fly very well. It sticks the back of its body out of the water at short intervals to take in oxygen.*

*3. **Smooth newt** (Trituris vulgaris). Prefers areas of ponds that are full of plants and weed. Will also live in streams. Lives on insects, earthworms and small water creatures. Overwinters on land.*

*4. **Common frog** (Rana temporaria). Likes living in company; can often be seen sunbathing. Lives on insects, worms, snails and small invertebrates. Overwinters in the pond.*

*5. **The pond skater** (Gerris lacustris) lives on the surface of the water. It moves in a jerky, staggered way when hunting its prey – small insects that have fallen into the water. Overwinters on land.*

*6. **Common backswimmer** or **water boatman** (Notonecta glauca). Swims on its back; flies very well. Lives on small water creatures and fish fry. Overwinters in the pond.*

*7. **Swan mussel** (Anodonta cygnaea). The largest European freshwater pond mussel. Lives on tiny creatures which it filters out of the water. It provides a spawning place and nursery for bitterling. Overwinters in the pond.*

*8. **Common toad** (Bufo bufo). The most common species of toad. Overwinters on land.*

Feeding the fish: You can feed them several times a day, but only offer as much food as they will eat right away. The food should never end up sinking to the bottom of the pond.
● Give the food slowly and in small quantities, so that you can see if the fish really eat it all.
● Never give them extra food. Even if you have forgotten to feed them for two or three days, the fish will not starve to death. The pond contains plenty of food.
Important: As soon as the temperature of the water drops below 12°C (54°F), you will have to stop feeding (see overwintering, p. 41).
Refusal to feed: If the fish sometimes refuse to take the food, do not worry. They have probably stuffed themselves on food that occurs naturally in their pond (insects, plants). However, note how long they refuse to take fish food. Refusal to eat can be a symptom of disease!

Sick fish

Fish will rarely become ill in a well-cared-for pond. However, organisms that cause disease can be brought to the pond by newly bought fish, or by birds or insects that have also visited an infested pond in your neighbourhood.

Fungi and parasites
About 90% of all diseases in garden-pond fish are due to fungi or parasites.
Symptoms: Fungal infections are characterized by cotton-wool-like layers on the body or fins. Parasites show as whitish, spotted, rice-grain-like attachments or cloudy-looking skin; the fish can be seen rubbing against plant stalks and showing oddly uncoordinated movements and will refuse to feed.

Treatment: You should be able to obtain the right medication from aquarium suppliers or a vet, who will be pleased to advise you if you describe the symptoms you have observed as exactly as possible.
Care of sick fish: The fish should always be treated in the pond. A sick fish may have already infected others without your knowledge, so the entire pond has to be treated. Naturally, dead fish should be removed at once.
How to treat fish: Before putting the medication into the water, change half of the water.
● Treat the fresh water carefully; treatment agents can be obtained from aquarium suppliers.
● Make sure additional oxygen is provided with the help of an air pump or an oxygenator.
● Check that the filter is in good working order.
● Do not feed the fish for a week.
● When using medication, stick to the instructions given.
Following treatment:
● Do not immediately change the water. Wait for about a fortnight, then change a maximum of one-third of the water three times at intervals of one week.
● Prepare the fresh water with only half of the recommended dose of medication (read the instructions).
Warning: Never put cooking salt or lime into the pond! These old home remedies will endanger life in the whole pond.

Making visitors welcome

The garden pond and marginal area will provide food and shelter for many animals. However, you can do a little more for these visitors to your pond if you make the vicinity compatible with the lifestyle of amphibians (frogs, newts and toads), birds and insects. A few simple measures will help.
Dead twigs: Pile up large and small branches and twigs near the bank, with dead leaves, grass cuttings and compost on top. This will provide a hiding place for frogs, newts and toads, which only spend part of their time in the water during their reproductive cycle. Here they will find rich pickings in the way of earthworms and insects.
Hedgehogs will also be grateful for a home in a pile of dead twigs and leaves.
Stones and rotting pieces of wood: If left near a pond or in a quiet spot in the garden, these will attract visitors to your garden pond.
Bird bath: What would a garden be without birds? Choose a clear space for the bird bath. There should be no shrubs or bushes in the immediate vicinity of it because when birds are drinking or bathing they become so preoccupied that they often relax their natural watchfulness and may easily fall prey to a cat lurking in the nearby bushes.
Protection of amphibians: You can obtain detailed information on the protection of toads and other amphibians from local nature protection groups or books on the care and protection of amphibians.

Index

Figures in bold indicate illustrations.

Index

Index

Cover photographs

Front cover main picture: *A very small pond with small waterlily Nymphaea odorata minor*; top right: *Pig's-head water feature creates a stir*; middle right: *The lively addition of falling water*; bottom right: *A duck at home in a large garden pond.* Inside front cover: *Pond with water lilies and purple loosestrife.* Inside back cover: *Nature pond with yellow irises in the foreground.* Back cover: *A raised sink pond with water spout, gunnera, ferns and clematis.*

Photographic acknowledgements

Becker: 7 (Gartenarchitekt: Horst Schummelfelder), 26 (Gartenarchitektin: Mary Baumeister); Burda/Mein Schöner Garten: inside back cover; Busek: 3 top right, 20; Eisenbeiss: 2, 17, 51; John Glover, Garden Picture Library: front cover main picture, back cover; Hagemann: 58 no. 1; Kahl: 54, 56 no. 2; Konig: 8 bottom; Pforr: 34 no. 6, 40 bottom and top, 58 no. 2; Pott: 58 nos 6 and 8; Reinhard: 33 no. 5, 56 no. 1, 5 and 6; Riedmiller: 34 no. 1; Ruckstuhl: 8 top, 58 no. 4; Scherz: 34 no. 5; Schlaback: inside front cover (Gartenarchitekt: Henk Weijers); Silvestris: 56 no.4; Stehling: 44, 45; Graham Strong: front cover top, middle and bottom right; Wothe: 58 no. 5; Zeininger: 56 no. 3, 58 nos 3 and 7; Strauss: all other photos.

This edition published 1999 by
Merehurst Limited
Ferry House, 51–57 Lacy Road,
Putney, London SW15 1PR

© 1989 Gräfe und Unzer GmbH, Munich

ISBN 1-85391-754-0

English text copyright ©
Merehurst Limited 1994
Translated by Astrid Mick
Edited by Lesley Young
Design/typesetting by
Cooper Wilson Design
Illustrations by Fritz W. Köhler
Printed in Hong Kong by Wing King Tong